# *Kingdom*
# *Citizens*

# *Kingdom Citizens*

**John Driver**

**Introduction by
Donald B. Kraybill**

**HERALD PRESS**
Scottdale, Pennsylvania
Kitchener, Ontario
1980

**Library of Congress Cataloging in Publication Data**

Driver, John, 1924-
    Kingdom citizens.

    1.Sermon on the mount. 2. Christian life—
Mennonite authors. 3. Christian life—Biblical
teaching. I. Title.
BT380.2.D72      226'.906      80-16171
ISBN 0-8361-1935-5 (pbk.)

KINGDOM CITIZENS
Copyright © 1980 by Herald Press, Scottdale, Pa. 15683
    Published simultaneously in Canada by Herald Press
    Kitchener, Ont. N2G 4M5
Library of Congress Catalog Card Number: 80-16171
International Standard Book Number: 0-8361-1935-5
Printed in the United States of America
Design: Alice B. Shetler

15   14   13   12   11   10   9   8   7   6   5   4   3   2   1

To brothers and sisters in the
Christain community in Horta
(Barcelona, Spain) in whose
fellowship the grace of God is
simply amazing!

# Contents

# Introduction

In *Kingdom Citizens* the author invites us to climb the Mount and reflect once again on Jesus' sermon. John Driver is a skillful tour guide on the climb up this theological mountain. He points out the surrounding landscape and helps us observe the sayings of Jesus in their social and political context. A host of theological battles down through the centuries have been fought over the words of Jesus which are deposited on this mound. Driver reminds us of these battles and reviews the significant issues that generated the combat.

It soon becomes clear that there are many perspectives from which one can view this mountain. The author gives us some equipment—keys of interpretation as he calls them—for climbing the mountain. Interestingly, in Matthew's version Driver observes three peaks on this mountain and carefully assists us in scaling each of them.

Boldly this mountain of thought juts out against the surrounding cultural landscape of yesterday and today. It points us toward a new value system that undergirds the kingdom of God. John Driver reminds us that historically the churches have squabbled over the details of orthodox belief statements but have rarely given us concrete examples of what the Christian ethic of love might actually look like in action. On this climb we discover love-vignettes of the shape and form of kingdom behavior. These do not constitute a behavioral code which easily fits the multiplicity of our situations. Rather they provide glimpses and images of what the Christian way is all about.

Driver is a good guide. He's easy to follow and rarely gets lost. He speaks clearly and quickly and doesn't carry a lot of excess baggage in his backpack. He's straightforward and points out the way without leading us in circles.

Driver hopes that we won't see this trip as a short excursion—as just a little side trip from the press of our duties. I think he wants us to stay on the mountain. He'd be disappointed if we smiled politely at the sights, said "That's interesting," and then headed back home again. He invites us to become mountaineers.

Jesus' sermon embodies more than a utopian dream. Its lucid teaching is the bedrock of the kingdom. Our guide urges us to discard our tourist tags and take up residence on the mountain as *kingdom citizens*—persons who actually live the kingdom way.

It's a steep mountain. There are surprising turns in the path and many obstacles along the way. But we have a trustworthy guide. So come along and join us in an exciting climb.

*Donald B. Kraybill*
Elizabethtown, Pennsylvania

# Author's Preface

One of the signs of hope in our time is the emergence of movements within the traditional denominations, as well as among the so-called believers' churches, where conversion means first of all submission to the lordship of Jesus Christ in the context of the messianic community—with all that this signifies in terms of transformed values and radical changes in style of life.

This book follows the premise that for the New Testament community the point of reference in teaching new believer-disciples was instruction in the new life of the kingdom which had come in Jesus. Matthew, in his Gospel, places the summary which we know as the Sermon on the Mount at the beginning, immediately after the introductory material. This Gospel was written late in the first century to instruct new disciples of Jesus in the life of the messianic community. Other didactic material in the New Testament, particularly ethical teaching, is scattered throughout the kerygmatic material dedicated to the fundamental proclamation of the Messiah and His kingdom. Apparently these are the two centers around which the primitive apostolic message was oriented: Proclamation of the Messiah and His kingdom and teaching concerning the life which characterizes this kingdom.

It may be said without exaggeration that for a majority of

Christians in the West, the Christian life revolves primarily around sacraments and doctrine. The system of values of the larger society, at the same time, is structured so as to mesh with Christian faith, thereby altering or compromising that faith. In contrast, the messianic community which Jesus inaugurated sets a standard whereby life is lived according to a totally different set of values. This disparity may catch us unawares, especially in the tendency of the church to develop systems to fit faith together with the values of the larger society instead of seeing them stand in tension and even conflict.

By understanding "belief" as intellectual assent, and "conversion" as a change of intellectual or idealogical orientation, many evangelical churches of our time have continued to narrow the gospel in order to facilitate entrance into the church. But in doing so, they have stripped these concepts of their biblical content in which "belief" carries a sense of commitment, loyalty, and obedience, and "conversion" refers to a radical reorientation which places a person within the stream of the messianic community.

To the degree to which the church rediscovers the roots of its life and mission in the world, to that degree will it be liberated from the sterility of those definitions of the Christian life in terms of sacraments, and from the equally paralyzing limitations of mere correct doctrinal formulations. Only by returning to its authentic roots in the New Testament will the church be able to free itself from a millstone fastened around its neck which threatens to destroy it. To live up to the biblical faith it proclaims and to live out the promise of that singular claim is the challenge which faces the church.

This book is designed to accompany and orient direct study of the Sermon on the Mount. The study abounds in biblical references which throw additional light on the text and aid in its interpretation. Its study is recommended to those who desire a life of discipleship which corresponds more nearly to God's intention for His community of salvation. Inasmuch as readers are moved to take new steps of commitment and obedience to the will of God as this has been most clearly revealed to us in the person of the Messiah, this book will have fulfilled its purpose.

Most of the material which is offered in the following pages has been shared with fellow disciples on two continents. The outline has been expanded considerably since it was first used at youth retreats in Cachipay, Colombia, and Trenque Lauquen, Argentina. In fuller form it has been shared with university students in the summer seminar of the Spanish chapter of Inter-Varsity held near Valencia, Spain, as well as with congregations in Barcelona and Madrid, Spain.

Before taking up this book, I would encourage readers to read and re-read the biblical text found in Matthew 1 to 7; indeed to first read all of Matthew. Then read Matthew alongside this book. Test what you read. May the Spirit guide you to new joy in living in the community of Christ's kingdom.

I take this occasion to thank all of these brothers and sisters who have enriched my understanding of the gospel of Jesus Christ as we have shared in a common study of the Word. My obvious indebtedness to John W. Miller's *The Christian Way* (Herald Press, 1969), as well as to other teachers in the church, is gratefully recognized.

# *Kingdom Citizens*

# Chapter 1

# The Setting of the Sermon on the Mount

In order to understand the Sermon on the Mount, we must view it within the setting of Matthew's Gospel. The first Gospel has often been called the "Gospel of the Kingdom" because this seems to be the underlying theme. In this connection the message enunciated in Matthew 4:17 is of fundamental importance: "From that time Jesus began to preach, saying, 'Repent, for the kingdom of heaven is at hand.' " With these words Jesus declares that already, in His own person, the sovereign reign of God has become an earthly reality (Matthew 12:28).

*Jesus fulfills Old Testament promises and types*
*Jesus and the new creation* (Matthew 1). Matthew begins his Gospel by asserting that the appearance of Jesus of Nazareth in human history inaugurates a new era, or more precisely, initiates a new creation. The first verse of the Gospel begins: "The book of the genealogy of Jesus Christ." Actually the Greek of this verse translated literally means "the book of the *genesis* of Jesus Christ." While this word can also mean "genealogy," in the way that Matthew uses the term here it probably means "generation" or "beginning." We should understand it as a reference to the beginning found in the Old Testament, to the "first" book of

Genesis, to the generation of the universe itself (Genesis 2:4), or to the beginning or genesis of the first Adam (Genesis 5:1).

The evangelist has undoubtedly begun his Gospel with a phrase intended to suggest a parallel between Jesus and the first Adam, and even more, with the creation of the universe. The coming of Jesus means the inauguration of a new creation. Matthew would have us to understand that his Gospel is fundamentally a gospel of the new creation, or the new genesis.

In the genealogical table which begins with Abraham, Matthew places Jesus within the history of the people of God (1:1-17). But the form which the genealogy takes indicates that Matthew has another purpose in mind. Of the entire list, three persons are singled out for special attention: Abraham, David the king, and Jesus, who is called Christ or Messiah (1:1, 2, 6, 16, 17). Among all of the kings listed, Matthew assigns royal titles to only two: David (1:6) and Jesus (1:1, 16, 17). Apparently Matthew's purpose is to show that Jesus, descendant of both David and Abraham, is the heir of the promise which God made to the patriarch (Genesis 12:3; Galatians 3:16), but above all, he is the heralded "son of David." By his use of this title Matthew announces that the messianic king of Jewish expectation, the agent of God in the messianic age, has in reality appeared in the person of Jesus of Nazareth.

In his narration of the birth of Jesus (1:18-25) Matthew adds several elements of importance for a fuller understanding of the real nature of the person and mission of the Messiah. The same Holy Spirit of God, once active in the creation of the universe and in the salvation of the people of God throughout their history, plays the essential role in the appearance of Jesus, the inaugurator of the creation of the new people of God (1:18, 20). "You shall call his name Jesus," in its Hebrew form, means God saves. And this is precisely what is about to happen. Jesus "will save his people from their sins" (1:20). In the coming of Jesus the hopes of God's people are being fulfilled. God Himself is intervening in behalf of His people. In the person of His Messiah, God Himself is present in the midst of His people to succor and to save them (1:23).

*Jesus and kingship* (Matthew 2). In chapter 2 Matthew presents Jesus in relation to the sociopolitical framework of His time. Two times within the first four verses Matthew places Jesus in juxtaposition with Herod. This confrontation, together with the emphasis placed on the political titles assigned to each, generally escapes our notice when we read the story of the visit of the wise men from the East from the perspective of the church's traditional Christmas liturgy. Within the boundaries of the territory in which "Herod the king" (2:1) exercised his sovereignty, One who is called "king of the Jews" (2:2) is born. Deeply troubled, Herod the king (2:3) consults the Jewish religious leaders in relation to the birth of "the Christ" (2:4). In first-century Palestine "Christ," or messiah, was a title which carried political connotations.

In his narrative describing the slaughter of the innocents (2:16), Matthew forcefully calls attention to the fact that, for Herod the Great, this juxtaposition of kings (2:1-4) is more than a mere grammatical coincidence. Even the passage from the prophet Micah (Micah 5:2, 4), quoted by the religious leaders, which announced the coming of a ruler who would "shepherd" the people of God and who would be at the same time their "peace" (5:5a), did not quiet Herod's suspicions. Matthew reports knowingly that Herod "was troubled, and all Jerusalem with him" (2:3). In all probability the people expected that Herod would react violently to this news. Just as they had feared, in keeping with the proverbial Herodian character, violence was not long in coming. The presence of another king within the confines of the kingdom of Herod constituted a political threat which he was not willing to tolerate. This king must therefore be eliminated.

*Jesus the new Moses* (Matthew 2:13-18). Matthew sees in Jesus not only the inaugurator of a new creation and the messianic king, the heralded "son of David." He also presents Jesus as the new Moses (21:11; Deuteronomy 18:15, 19). One parallel between the life of Jesus and Moses is found in the massacres of the male children by Pharaoh when the first Moses was born and by Herod when Jesus was born (2:13-18). Moses played a funda-

mental role in Judaism. He was a veritable colossus: the liberator
who led his people from slavery to freedom, the mediator of the
law which was commonly regarded in Judaism as the final revelation of God. But now Matthew reveals that a new Moses, the true
liberator of His people, the bearer of the ultimate revelation of
God, has appeared in human history.

*Jesus and the new Israel* (Matthew 2:14). Matthew not only
points to a correspondence between Jesus and Moses, but also
between Jesus and the new Israel (Matthew 2:14). He describes
the flight into Egypt and the subsequent return in the words of
the prophet, "Out of Egypt have I called my son" (Hosea 11:1;
Exodus 4:22). While the Old Testament writers referred to Israel
as God's son, Matthew perceives in the person of Jesus the coming
into being of the new Israel which supersedes the old.

*Jesus the new prophet* (Matthew 3). In chapter 3 Matthew
places Jesus, together with John the Baptist, in the venerable
prophetic tradition of the Hebrews (Matthew 5:12). In fact, one
almost receives the impression that the gospel of Jesus is already
present incipiently in the ministry of John. As Matthew records
them, the messages of John the Baptist and Jesus are identical:
"Repent, for the kingdom of heaven is at hand" (3:2; 4:17). But
Jesus was not merely another disciple of John; quite to the
contrary, John is presented as a servant-disciple of Jesus (3:11, 14).
While John was the last and the greatest of Hebrew prophets,
clearly Jesus is more than a prophet.

John's message of repentance consisted of an invitation to a
radically new orientation in terms of life and values. It involved
considerably more than mere change of mind. It meant returning
to the roots—a return to God and to His intention for humanity as
expressed in the covenant which He had made with His people
and was now about to make anew in the person of His Messiah
coming to inaugurate His kingdom. It meant radical change
(from *radix*, the Latin term for root). So repentance has to do with
really fundamental changes which affect the roots of social relationships. It is the absolutely essential condition for participation
in the new messianic kingdom.

Luke alone includes in his Gospel a passage which provides a more explicit description of the concrete social content of repentance (3:10-14). For the people in general it meant sharing clothing and food with those in need. None should possess more than they need while others lack (3:10, 11). For tax collectors repentance meant not collecting more than the stipulated amount. In other words, they should be honest as well as have compassion on those who were struggling under an exorbitant tax burden (3:12, 13). For soldiers, who in this case were probably guards who accompanied the tax collectors in order to enforce the collection of public funds, repentance meant abandoning their violent, bullying methods for extorting payment (3:14).

So repentance was not a matter of "hair shirts and ashes"; nor was it a question of "doing penance." In reality it had to do with a return to the concrete practice of justice in social relationships which responds to God's original intention for humanity. To imagine changes more fundamental than these is difficult: avarice and selfishness are converted into generosity; dishonesty, fraudulence, and lack of personal compassion are transformed into sincerity, integrity, and compassion; and the violence and bullying tactics of the soldiers are changed into respect for others.

*Jesus the Messiah: announcing the coming of the messianic kingdom.* The message of John the Baptist, as well as that of Jesus, has to do with a radically new reality, the messianic kingdom. All images converge in the image of Jesus as messiah, the announcer of the new messianic kingdom. This radical newness is reflected in the figures which John employs in his preaching. True children of Abraham will participate in the life of the new kingdom. And in the absence of authentic repentance on the part of those who presume to have Abraham as their father, God will be able "from these stones to raise up children to Abraham" (Matthew 3:9).

The presence of the messianic kingdom constitutes a judgment: "Every tree therefore that does not bear good fruit is cut down and thrown into the fire" (3:10). "Even now the axe is laid to the root of the trees" (3:10). The message of John points toward social structures of radically new dimensions. It is directed toward the formation of a new human society. The new humanity of the kingdom will now become a glorious possibility because the Messiah is about to appear. He "will baptize with the Holy Spirit and with fire" (3:11), with power to both purify and to make alive.

### Announcing Jesus' messianic mission

Chapter 3 ends with a message from God Himself: "This is my beloved Son, with whom I am well pleased" (3:17). Jesus undoubtedly recognized in these words well-known texts from the Old Testament. One of these texts comes from a messianic vision in which God promises the "Son": "I will make the nations your heritage . . . you shall break them with a rod of iron" (Psalms 2:7-9). (The allusion to Psalm 2 is even clearer in Luke 3:22, where the voice from heaven says: "*Thou art* my beloved Son.") The other text is found in the prophetic vision of the suffering servant of Yahweh, who "will not cry or lift up his voice, or make it heard in the street; a bruised reed he will not break, and a dimly burning wick he will not quench"; however, "he will faithfully bring forth justice" (Isaiah 42:1-4). What do these words mean to Jesus at this crucial moment in His messianic mission?

In the first place, Jesus surely recognized in these words a divine messianic commission. His Father was calling Him to be His Messiah in the world. Therefore these words should probably be understood in relation to the character of Jesus' mission in the world, rather than as a metaphysical description of His relationship with the Father. The concern in the history of the church to understand the divinity of Jesus in relation to His humanity is, of course, comprehensible. But in this particular text the question under consideration is this: What kind of *man* does the Father want His Messiah to be in the world?

Second, the juxtaposition of the two different messianic visions places squarely before Jesus the necessity of deciding what kind of messiah He is going to be. Will He exercise royal power according to the vision reflected in the messianic psalm, forcibly imposing His authority over people from the beginning of His earthly ministry? Or is the will of God for His Messiah the salvation of His people by means of suffering servanthood, as described in the prophetic vision of Isaiah 42? How is Jesus to understand the will of God in the fulfillment of His messianic mission?

*The times: religious and political options*

The social and political situation in first-century Palestine was characterized by its turbulence. Palestine was but one colony among many which formed part of the vast Roman Empire, and as such it suffered from all of the evils which are inherent in these situations: foreign oppression symbolized by the omnipresence of the forces of occupation, the much feared Roman legions; a complex system of taxation which kept a large portion of the population in economic misery; injustices and violence, institutional and official violence as well as revolutionary violence and terrorism.

As can be expected in situations such as these, people tend to polarize around a variety of different political options. And this is exactly what happened in first-century Palestine. While the situation was complex, probably four principle social alternatives existed.

*Prudent collaboration: Sadducees and Herodians.* One of these options might be described as the strategy of prudent collaboration. The Sadducees and the Herodians in the New Testament fall into this category. They apparently felt that it was wise to collaborate with the imperial power in what they understood to be the best interests of the Jewish people. With this strategy they were able to salvage a number of benefits. They retained control of the temple, as well as the privilege of determining their own religious life and practice (something few of the conquered nations within the Roman Empire achieved). Roman symbols were removed from Jerusalem due to the Jewish opposition to images.

The stance of the Sadducees and Herodians basically called for making the best of a bad situation. Matthew himself, as a tax collector, may have shared this political view. This philosophy led the High Priest Caiaphas to declare, "It is expedient for you that one man should die for the people, and that the whole nation should not perish" (John 11:49, 50). Of course, he said this without first asking if Jesus was innocent or guilty because he was not especially interested in doing justice in particular cases. Caiaphas was more interested in obtaining the greatest possible benefit (as he understood it) for the largest number of people. His was the policy of expediency. Needless to say, this strategy did not interest Jesus.

*Withdrawal and retreat: Essenes.* Another of the political options of the period was the strategy of withdrawal and retreat. This was the alternative of the Essenes. They categorically refused to collaborate with the system as it was organized under the Roman Empire. Therefore they withdrew to the desert and there formed their own separatist communities. There they were able to keep the commandments of Yahweh without compromise or conflict. In spite of their geographical isolation, they were able to make a positive contribution to Jewish society. The scrolls which they produced are among the best commentaries and manuscripts of Old Testament literature. These are the well-known Dead Sea Scrolls found in the caves of Qumran.

Of course, we need not withdraw to the desert in order to take the alternative of the Essenes. It is possible to isolate oneself in the modern city and to withdraw from the conflicts and problems of society. The Essenes were not as apolitical as they might appear. They evidently awaited the day when Yahweh would intervene in the affairs of mankind and establish His justice. Meanwhile they lived expectantly. Although in terms of strategy this alternative did not appear to be politically successful, it was a position characterized by a certain coherence, and it proved attractive to a number of serious and committed persons. If Jesus had taken the alternative which the Essenes offered, He most certainly would not have died on a cross. But the spirit of the Essenes was not compatible to the spirit of Jesus.

*Symbolic separation: Pharisees.* A third option is one that we might call a strategy of symbolic separation. This is the alternative adopted by the Pharisees. They lived in society, participating in the social, economic, and political aspects of life as far as they deemed it was necessary. They established rules of conduct whereby they might live a life of purity in the midst of a situation characterized by impurity. They, together with other Jews of their time, hated the Roman military presence which profaned their holy places and restricted their personal liberty, and they refused to touch the Roman coins which bore the image of Caesar. But this did not keep them from reaping as many benefits as possible from the things which this money could buy and the social situation which the exercise of this power could impose.

When all was said and done, the Pharisees' separation was largely spiritual and ritual, or religious. They were probably sincere in their attempt to reconcile collaborating with the unjust Roman system with the righteous demands of God's law. In the Gospels we note that Jesus shared certain aspects of their theological orientation. But He did not spare words in denouncing their hypocrisy, and He condemned them for their attempts to reduce God's righteousness to ritual practice. Jesus, with His clarity of thought and daring obedience, presented a threat to the precarious neutrality of the Pharisees.

*Revolutionary resistance: Zealots.* The fourth option was that taken by the Zealots. It was the strategy which called for the use of revolutionary violence. In reality it was a sort of national liberation movement organized to resist foreign aggression with armed force if necessary. In fact, between the years 50 BC and AD 125, an armed uprising occurred about every twenty years. We should remember that in addition to trusting the power of their own weapons, they also looked for a miraculous intervention of God in behalf of His people.

There were a number of similarities between the Zealot movement and the messianic movement which Jesus initiated. Jesus also advocated changes; in fact, He called for radical social changes. One also notes certain similarities in the language employed by both movements: messiah, kingdom of God, and so on. Of all places, one discovers in the song of Mary, the Magnificat, concepts which apparently express the aspirations of the Zealots as well (Luke 1:51-54). At least one of the twelve disciples, Simon, came from the ranks of the Zealot movement, and likely others were sympathetic toward this movement and its goals, as well as its methods. Peter was armed until the bitter end in Gethsemane, and his aspirations for the kind of messiah which he hoped Jesus would be may not have been too different at one time from theirs (Matthew 26:51, 52; 16:21-23). James and John, the "sons of thunder," showed a spirit similar to that of the Zealots in their attitude toward the unfriendly Samaritan villagers (Luke 9:54) and in their petition aimed at securing the two most important posts in the new regime they were expecting (Matthew 20:20-28).

It has been suggested that the Roman authorities probably thought that Jesus was a Zealot and for that reason had Him crucified. If this is true, they were, of course, wrong in their evaluation. But be all this as it may, of all the strategic alternatives which were available in first-century Palestine, the option of the Zealots probably presented the biggest temptation to Jesus. At least this is apparent in the temptation narrative in the Gospels.

### Options not taken

*The temptation narrative reflects what the messianic kingdom is not (Matthew 4:1-11).* Matthew records the temptations of Jesus in the first eleven verses of chapter 4. The Christian church has tended to see in this passage temptations to abuse the divine power which was at Jesus' disposal for selfish motives. But the context in which Matthew (and Luke) places the temptation narrative indicates that it is better to understand the passage in terms of messianic options. The tempter's phrase, "If you are the Son of God" (4:3, 6), should not be interpreted in terms of Jesus' metaphysical relationship with the Father, but rather in the sense of His messianic commission. It is as if the tempter had said to Jesus, "Since you are the Son of God (or, since you are the Messiah), command these stones to become loaves of bread" (4:3), and "since you are the Son of God, throw yourself down" (4:6). In the context of His messianic commission, Jesus' temptations have to do with the kind of messianic king He is going to be, as well as the methods He is going to employ to attain His goal.

*Not by bread alone.* In the first of the temptations Jesus is invited to become a Messiah who solves the economic problems of His people. We should probably not interpret this temptation as first and foremost an invitation to use His supernatural power to feed Himself. After all, one does not need a desert full of loaves to break a fast. Jesus was probably tempted to try to provide bread for His followers—to be an economic Messiah. Jesus rejected this alternative because He understood that the real needs of human-kind are much more inclusive. The concrete and total existence needs of people as the bearers of God's image cannot be satisfied by bread alone (4:4).

In the Gospel of Luke we are told that the devil "departed from him until an opportune time" (4:13). And sure enough, later on the words of the tempter would prove to be right. When Jesus fed the five thousand in the desert, the multitude tried to "take him by force to make him king" (John 6:14, 15). And Jesus was able to save Himself from this threat only by escaping to the hills.

*Not by supernatural feats.* In the second temptation Jesus is invited to leap from the pinnacle of the temple into the square below. Jesus rejected this temptation because it was out of harmony with the real nature of God (4:5-7). To attempt such a feat would amount to tempting God. Again, instead of seeing in this temptation another invitation to use His supernatural power to work miracles, it is probably better to interpret it in the light of the messianic commission which Jesus had received. In the Hebrew tradition was a prophetic vision of the "messenger of the covenant" appearing "suddenly" in the temple for the purpose of purifying His people (Malachi 3:1-4). Undoubtedly Jesus is here being tempted to be this heavenly messenger from above who appears suddenly in the temple square. He is tempted to play the role of the religious reformer who establishes Himself in a sort of supernatural political and religious coup. Jesus' sudden and inexplicable appearance in the center of the social and religious life of Judaism could well be the sure sign that the promised Messiah had arrived.

Later on in the life of Jesus this temptation presented itself anew in a somewhat different form. The triumphal procession into Jerusalem during which Jesus was proclaimed the messianic messenger, "Hosanna to the Son of David," reached its climax in the temple square. (In this context we should remember that "Hosanna to the Son of David! Blessed is he who comes in the name of the Lord! Hosanna in the highest!" is a clear reference to Psalm 118:25, 26, a liturgical text which was well known in Israel. And the term "hosanna" is not a mere messianic acclamation otherwise void of meaning. It literally means "free us" or "save us." The political, as well as religious, meaning of this public manifestation would have been obvious.) The authorities were apparently unable (or unwilling) to keep Jesus from driving out "all who sold and bought in the temple." Now in the social and religious center of Judaism the moment suggested by the tempter had arrived again. But Jesus knew that taking over the temple square by force was not consistent with the messianic path which the Father had placed before Him. Therefore Jesus abandoned the temple and, turning His back on the multitude, He withdrew to Bethany (Matthew 21:12-17).

*Not by a show of strength.* The messianic character of the third temptation has generally been recognized. The voice from heaven had quoted Psalm 2:7, "You are my son." And now the tempter apparently quotes the promise which follows: "Ask of me, and I will make the nations your heritage, and the ends of the earth your possession" (2:8). "All the kingdoms of the world and the glory of them" will belong to Jesus if He will only bow His knee before the tempter. Instead of imagining some sort of satanic cult, it would be more nearly in line with the messianic context of this passage to observe that in this temptation Jesus recognizes the idolatrous character of the desire to exercise economic, political, and military power. People have sometimes asked if Satan was really in a position to offer the "kingdoms of the world" to Jesus. But the ability or inability of Satan to deliver them really has nothing to do with the reason for which Jesus rejected the offer. He refused because the exercise of secular power which depends on economic wealth, on political prowess, and on military force contradicts diametrically the nature of Jesus' messianic mission in the world. Jesus opted rather for the messianic vision of Isaiah— the vision of the suffering servant of Yahweh.

This same temptation, the establishment of the kingdom through the exercise of violence, later presented itself to Jesus on more than one occasion. When Peter tried to persuade Jesus to abandon the path of suffering servanthood, Jesus recognized in his attitude another version of the old satanic temptation. This explains the energetic response of Jesus to Peter: "Get behind me, Satan! You are a hindrance to me; for you are not on the side of God, but of men" (Matthew 16:23). On this occasion Peter represents the same diabolic temptation which Jesus had turned down in the desert with the same exclamation, "Begone, Satan!" (In the Greek text of Matthew 4:10 and 16:23 the verbs employed are identical.) Later still, in Gethsemane, the possibility of appealing to the Father for "more than twelve legions of angels" to wage a holy war aimed at the establishment of the kingdom represented yet another version of the same temptation (Matthew 26:52, 53).

*Common theme.* All of the temptations with which Jesus struggled represented some aspect of the nationalistic messianic expectations which a good part of the Jewish people of the first century shared. Apparently Jesus' disciples themselves also shared, in one form or another, this nationalistic vision. James and John asked for places of power in the new regime (Matthew 20:20-28). Peter surely spoke for the entire group when he tried to persuade Jesus to abandon the strategy of salvation through suffering (Matthew 16:22). Until the end the disciples kept asking Jesus if He wasn't going to "restore the kingdom to Israel" in their time (Acts 1:6).

*The alternative: the nature of the messianic king/kingdom*
*The Messiah as servant (Matthew 4:12-25).* Jesus adopted a different kind of messianic strategy. Rather than allowing Himself to be forced into one of the messianic molds of the time, Jesus had a different understanding of the Father's will. Taking His cue

from the voice from heaven, Jesus understood His commission in terms of the true servant of Yahweh as announced by the prophet Isaiah (42:1). In light of this vision, Matthew's narration in the remaining verses of chapter 4 of the steps which Jesus took is comprehensible.

Matthew reports that Jesus begins at this point to announce the gospel of the kingdom. "From that time Jesus began to preach, saying, 'Repent, for the kingdom of heaven is at hand.' . . . And he went about all Galilee, teaching in their synagogues and preaching the gospel of the kingdom" (Matthew 4:17, 23). The meaning of repentance in the preaching of Jesus is undoubtedly the same as in the preaching of John the Baptist (Matthew 3:2). It is essentially an invitation to a radical return to the covenant which Yahweh in His gracious love established with His people. This has been continually violated by disobedience and broken trust, but repentance is a return to the roots of our salvation, a return to the intention of God for the life of His people.

Biblical repentance does not turn a person inward (introversion) upon self and faults. It is a return which has little in common with mere remorse, or twinges of conscience, or simply feeling bad about one's faults. It is a radical return to God and to His will for humankind expressed originally in His good creation, reiterated in His gracious covenant at Sinai, and finally manifested with radiant clarity in the person of His Messiah.

Fundamental changes such as these, of course, will lead to the formation of a new kind of society. They are the prelude to the reconstitution of the people of God gathered around His Messiah. For this reason Matthew points out that the message of Jesus is "the gospel of the kingdom" (4:23). The gospel which Jesus brings is essentially the good news that the kingdom (or reign) of God is to be established among humankind.

This kingdom of God which Jesus proclaims (Matthew uses the "kingdom of heaven" in his Gospel, probably due to the Jewish reticence to speak the divine name) has to do with the establishment of the sovereign authority of God among people on earth. Although it is certainly true that God reigns over the entire universe, the point of Jesus' declaration here is that the King intervenes with saving purpose in the history of humanity. In the person of His Messiah, God is now acting in a decisive and definitive way which brings together and completes His previous interventions through His messengers. In fact, this intervention in the person of His Messiah anticipates the fulfillment of God's purpose at the end of history.

This announcement of the arrival of the kingdom was a theme which intensely interested the Jews of the first century. Life moved along in the midst of heightened messianic expectations. The Jewish people were nourished by the hope that God would soon intervene in behalf of Israel, fulfilling the promises He had made through His prophets. Therefore the announcement of John the Baptist, as well as the proclamation of Jesus, alerted the people to the imminence of God's intervention. In Matthew's Gospel the narrative is seasoned with clear references to the way in which Jesus' life and ministry were fulfilling the ancient prophetic hopes for Israel. An understanding of the messianic kingdom which becomes a reality in the coming of Jesus Christ is fundamental for understanding the messianic ethic described in the Sermon on the Mount in terms of kingdom righteousness.

*The Messiah as healer and restorer.* Matthew points out that besides teaching in the synagogues and preaching the gospel of the kingdom, Jesus "went about . . . healing every disease and infirmity among the people" (4:23, 24). Jesus' healing ministry shows that He is, in truth, the One who is authorized by the Father to announce and to inaugurate the kingdom of heaven (Matthew 9:6, 11:2-6; 12:28; Luke 11:20). These healings and exorcisms do not set Jesus apart merely as a miracle worker of extraordinary power, but are primarily indications of the *kind* of messiah that He has become. To the query of John the Baptist, "Are you he who is to come, or shall we look for another?" the answer of Jesus consists of pointing to His messianic activity. "Go tell John what you hear and see: the blind receive their sight and the lame walk, lepers are cleansed and the deaf hear, and the dead are raised up, and the poor have good news preached to them"

(Matthew 11:4, 5). This is not a veiled answer to John's question. Quite to the contrary, it is a clear answer. Yes, Jesus is the One "who is to come." He is the One who, since His baptism at the hands of John, has been commissioned to be precisely this kind of Messiah (Matthew 3:17; Isaiah 42:1-4).

So the healing ministry of Jesus is in reality messianic activity. While it did not conform to the nationalist political hopes of a good part of the Jewish people of the period, it did correspond to the messianic vision reflected in the songs of the suffering servant of Yahweh of the Prophet Isaiah (42, 49, 50, 53). This is the way in which the New Testament writers interpreted the extraordinary healing ministry of Jesus (Matthew 8:17; 12:15-21; Acts 10:38). So Jesus is understood as the kind of Messiah who in truth bears the infirmities of the people, and His healings are signs that the Kingdom of God has arrived in His person.

In response to the people's question, "Can this be the Son of David?" and the negative conclusion of the Pharisees, Jesus declares, "If it is by the Spirit of God that I cast out demons, then the kingdom of God has come upon you" (Matthew 12:22-28; Luke 11:20). Matthew presents Jesus not only as the Messiah who teaches with authority, but also as the Messiah who makes persons whole in the power of the Spirit of God. His healings and exorcisms, then, are signs that the Kingdom of God is in their midst. In fact, immediately following the Sermon on the Mount, Matthew dedicates two chapters (8 and 9) to narrating these messianic works of Jesus.

*The Messiah as Creator of new humanity.* Jesus begins to invite persons to leave their occupations and voluntarily follow Him (Matthew 4:18-25). In this way Matthew describes the beginning of the formation of the new people of God, followers of His Messiah. Although Matthew mentions only four in this passage, the group will eventually number twelve, a fact which is certainly no mere accident, because these twelve represent the twelve tribes of Israel. These constitute the New Israel.

In Ephesians 2 we read of the creation of a "new humanity" in the messianic era which is made up of persons who are different from one another, in fact, who are even mutually antagonistic, but who are reconciled with one another and with God through the work of Jesus the Messiah. In the primitive community of the twelve this new social reality has already become concrete. What is really novel and revolutionary about this new community is the fact that ex-Zealots and ex-Herodians (former enemies) become co-participants in a movement in which the peace and justice of God, before sought after in such diverse ways, are finally realized. It is a community in which all of those barriers which usually separate persons into categories of personal enmity are overcome through the reconciling work of Jesus Christ. This is the new humanity, the messianic community created by Jesus Christ among His followers, the truly revolutionary new social reality which furnishes the context in which the Sermon on the Mount is comprehensible.

*Jesus, the new covenant maker.* We have already alluded to the fact that in his Gospel Matthew presents Jesus as the new Moses. In contrast to the mosaic covenant made at Sinai, Jesus establishes the new covenant (Matthew 26:28). For Matthew, as well as for the early church generally, the messianic era is a new Exodus wrought by Jesus as the new Moses. In Matthew 28:16-20 the Messiah as risen Lord commissions His people and then goes before them in their mission "to the close of the age." In Matthew 5:1, 2 it is the Messiah, as the new Moses on a new Sinai (i.e., "mountain"), whose description of life in the new messianic community points back to, but supersedes, the intention of God expressed on tablets of stone at the former Sinai.

While the figure of the new Moses is only one of several images employed by Matthew to portray Jesus, and by itself cannot reflect all of the full-orbed meaning of His messiahship, its thrust in Matthew's Gospel is inescapable. God, whose intention for the life of His people was once chiseled in stone and mediated by the first Moses, and who many times spoke through His prophets, is finally and fully revealing Himself and His will in the person and words and works of His Messiah, the new Moses (Hebrews 1:1-4).

### The setting in Matthew: structure of the Gospel

It should be pointed out that the Sermon on the Mount does not pretend to constitute the sum total of the Gospel. In fact, the form in which Matthew organized the material contained in the first of the Gospels appears to indicate this. The teachings of Jesus found in Matthew are presented in five discourses all containing insights into the nature of the kingdom of heaven. It is apparent that Matthew intentionally organized the teachings of Jesus in this way, since each of the five discourses ends with the identical formula (with minimal variations), "And when Jesus finished these sayings" (7:28; 11:1; 13:53; 19:1; 26:1).

The theme, of course, of the first of these discourses (the Sermon on the Mount) is the righteousness of the kingdom (chapters 5 to 7). The second deals with the mission of the messengers charged with proclaiming the kingdom (chapter 10). A collection of the parables of Jesus in chapter 13 reveals more fully the nature of the kingdom. Chapter 18 describes the way in which broken relationships among the followers of Jesus in the kingdom community are restored through forgiveness. And finally, in chapters 25 and 26, Jesus describes the way in which the kingdom, already inaugurated in His person, will be manifested in all of its fullness at the end of time. So in reality Matthew uses all five of the discourses of Jesus in his Gospel in order to present the gospel of the kingdom in its rich variety.

But in order to present even more clearly the gospel of the kingdom in his book, Matthew interweaves the series of discourses with narratives from the ministry of Jesus and finally ends his Gospel with the story of Jesus' Passion and resurrection. All of these words and deeds of Jesus are gospel and serve to further illuminate the kingdom of God and His righteousness described in the Sermon on the Mount. The writers of the New Testament are concerned to present the gospel of the kingdom in all of the rich implications of its inclusive character.

This, then, is the setting in which Matthew places the Sermon on the Mount in his Gospel. The principles of sound literary interpretation require us to take seriously the meaning of this setting. The kinds of relationships described in the Sermon on the Mount characterize the life of justice and peace in the kingdom of God which the Messiah has come to establish.

### Description of life in the messianic kingdom

The reign of God Himself was beginning in the person and ministry of Jesus. So the *imperative* of the Sermon on the Mount can be understood only within the context of the *indicative* of the inauguration of the kingdom. Since God has revealed His kingdom—His reign of salvation—in the person of His Messiah, all who enter His kingdom are called to the new messianic style of life—the righteousness of the kingdom. In the Sermon on the Mount we find the values and relationships which characterize this life described with transparent clarity. The Sermon on the Mount is a description of that life which corresponds to the kingdom of God.

We must also remember that a fundamental presupposition underlies each teaching in the Sermon on the Mount: the present evil age is passing away, and the age to come has already dawned. "The last days" of eschatological fulfillment have already begun with the appearing of the Messiah (Hebrews 1:2; *et al.*). The gospel of the kingdom is an invitation to return, through sincere repentance, to that life which responds to the intention of God, to live under His lordship. To be freed from the dominion of Satan is to live the life of the kingdom. In reality, *the life described in the Sermon on the Mount is the concrete form of the salvation which God offers to us through Jesus Christ.*

The life described in the Sermon on the Mount becomes a joyful possibility for all who participate in the kingdom of God, for those in whom the power of Satan has been broken through the grace of God, for those who have been baptized "with the Holy Spirit and with fire" (Matthew 3:11).

When we approach the Sermon on the Mount from the perspective of the kingdom of God and of the life which corresponds to that kingdom, we understand that the Sermon on the Mount is not complete. The teachings of Jesus contained in the

Sermon on the Mount do not pretend to order absolutely every aspect of the life of those who are subjects of the kingdom. Rather, they are instructions, which, although concrete, are representative; examples or signs which point to the way in which the life of the kingdom is lived in the midst of the world, the values of which correspond to the orientation of the evil one. In fact, the Golden Rule (Matthew 7:12) implies that many situations are not specifically covered by the instructions included in the Sermon on the Mount. However, the concrete meaning of these instructions and the direction in which the Sermon on the Mount points are abundantly clear.

While the Sermon on the Mount does not pretend to be a complete code of Christian ethics, in a sense its impact is quite complete, and even decisive. Here we refer to its revolutionary reordering of values. It offers a scale of values which stands over against all of the conventional value systems found in contemporary Judaism, in the Hellenistic and Roman cultures of the first century, and those which have characterized human societies since that time. In our own time this fundamental opposition is especially noticeable when we set the system of values which are both presupposed and proclaimed in the Sermon on the Mount over against the values which modern Western thought and culture take for granted.

The Sermon on the Mount declares that those who are really "blessed" are the ones who do not share the conventional values. The traditional norms for the determination of worth—wealth, social position, the exercise of personal or political power, even those personal achievements and possessions which are earned and defended by means of self-assertion and competitive rivalry— are all roundly repudiated. The fundamental opposition which we discover between the values of the kingdom and the value system which predominates in society in general underscores, among other things, that far from being a tentative formulation to govern the comportment of Christians, the Sermon on the Mount really constitutes a frontal challenge to all other systems of ethical values. This opposition is so radical that any attempts at adaptation or experiments in grafting the principles of the Sermon on the Mount into conventional systems of values in reality result in the repudiation of Jesus' teachings.

*Questions for Discussion*

1. What does the parallelism apparently intended by Matthew— (a) Moses and Jesus, (b) Israel and the new messianic people of God, and (c) the Sinaitic Law and the Sermon on the Mount—say to us regarding Jesus' intention for the Sermon on the Mount?

2. What does Luke 3:10-14 tell us about the biblical meaning of repentance?

3. What are the implications of Jesus' call to repentance? Was His invitation to repentance more radically concrete than John the Baptist's, or less so?

4. Does Matthew's description of Jesus' kingship give us any reason to think that His regime requires an allegiance which is more spiritual than it is concretely social and moral?

5. In what does the "radical newness" of the kingdom which Jesus announced consist?

6. Are Christians in our time tempted by the social alternatives of "prudent collaboration," "withdrawal," "symbolic separation," or "revolution"? Can you think of examples? Which has been your biggest temptation?

7. What was the social alternative which Jesus took? Do you know of Christians who are taking this alternative seriously?

8. Are the temptations which Jesus faced the kind which usually present themselves to religious leaders, or to political leaders? What does this tell us about the nature of Jesus' kingship and His kingdom? Does this have implications for our participation in Jesus' movement?

9. According to the New Testament, Jesus created a new kind of social reality, a "new humanity." Does the Christian congregation or community in which you participate show essential signs of being this new social reality? If not, what might be done about it?

10. Do you believe that the life described in the Sermon on the Mount is possible among God's people in our time? Why? What are the implications of your answer for the life of the church?

11. Do you think that the Sermon on the Mount is a fundamental part of the gospel? Or is biblical salvation possible independently of the values it sets forth?

# Chapter 2

# Historic Interpretation of the Sermon on the Mount

A widespread unwillingness in Christian circles to take the inauguration of the messianic kingdom as the fundamental point of departure for the interpretation of the Sermon on the Mount has led to a series of unfortunate deformations in the interpretation and practice of the church.

Much of the history of the Christian church is a story of attempts to patch old garments with pieces of "unshrunk cloth" and efforts to somehow "put new wine into old wineskins" (Matthew 9:16, 17). In reality it is a question of the values of "the age to come" (Hebrew 6:5) standing in frontal opposition to those values which characterize "the present evil age" (Galatians 1:4).

In the apostolic church the Sermon on the Mount was considered a point of departure instructing new followers of Jesus Christ. In fact it was a sort of catechism used for the instruction of new converts in the first century. However, in the subsequent history of the church, Christians have conceived of the Sermon on the Mount as the apogee of moral achievement toward which believers should strive. And furthermore, it came to be the common understanding that relatively few would reach this goal of so-called Christian perfection. The result of this reversal has been tragic within Christendom. The "righteousness" of much of

Christianity resembles that of the world which it tries to save, in some cases via the sacramental path, and in other cases via the path of faith without works. Unfortunately too often either approach amounts to little more than presumptuous credulity.

If the Christian church wants to survive the remaining years of the twentieth century as a messianic community which points to the kingdom, it has no other alternative than the one which the primitive apostolic community took: begin with the righteousness of the kingdom which is summed up in the Sermon on the Mount. The traditional interpretations to which the Sermon on the Mount has been subject in Christian history have proved themselves inadequate.

### Dualistic literalism

This method of interpreting the Sermon on the Mount takes the teachings of Jesus with literal seriousness. But it limits their application to a relatively small group within the larger church. Historically within the context of Roman Catholicism, religious orders—the Franciscans and others—have taken the Sermon on the Mount seriously. The demands of the Sermon on the Mount were understood to be counsels of perfection and therefore it was not expected that they could be applied to all of the members of the church. Only the more serious, or those who were aspiring to perfection, attempted to live according to these teachings.

This kind of ethical dualism can also be found in various forms among Protestant churches. Reinhold Niebuhr, North American Protestant ethicist, recognized that the sects (such as the historic Anabaptists) who take seriously the ethical demands of the Sermon on the Mount in reality play a prophetic role in the church. By their very presence they hold before the Christian church at large the ethical demands of the biblical ideal. However, it is generally understood that this is an impossible and irresponsible ideal for the majority of Christians. What Niebuhr and most mainline Christianity see is that Jesus was good, but he was not in a position to take responsibility for total society. Christians today, however, not only are in such a position, but should seize the opportunity for the sake of the good that can be done.

Another example of this ethical dualism which is found among evangelical groups can be seen in the fact that the moral expectations for the clergy are generally considerably higher than those which are applied to the laity.

However, it is surely doubtful that Jesus ever held this kind of dualistic understanding of the ethical practices of those who were participants in His kingdom. One does not discover in the New Testament a basis for two different levels of obedience within the community of the Messiah.

### An ethic of intention

This way of understanding the teachings of the Sermon on the Mount was suggested by the German theologian, Wilhelm Hermann, toward the end of the last century. In his attempt to free the Sermon on the Mount from all the vestiges of Jewish legalism he sought to emphasize the importance of the role of a person's intentions. He held that the ethical teachings of Jesus are directed principally to the inner spiritual disposition of a person, rather than to external acts of obedience. He taught that the teachings of Jesus are essentially spiritual in their intention.

There is certainly a sense in which our understanding of the response of a person to the demands of God was deepened by Jesus who underlined the importance of the inner motivation as well as the outward act. However, the antithesis which this interpretation formulates between the inner intention and the concrete acts of obedience is foreign both to the intention of Jesus and the spirit of the New Testament. The Sermon on the Mount is filled with instructions on how to act in situations which demand concrete obedience.

### Pedagogical interpretation

Instead of interpreting the Sermon on the Mount in terms of an ethic for disciples of the Messiah, this option interprets it in a theological or dogmatic sense. This understanding has been traditionally held among Lutherans, but has come to be quite common in most Protestant traditions. According to this view the teachings of Jesus are law. And the theological function of the law is peda-gogical. Our incapacity to keep the law teaches us to depend ex-clusively on grace for our salvation. And in response, God assures us of our salvation through His forensic justification. It is held that it was not Jesus' intention that the demands of the Sermon on the Mount be literally obeyed, because by definition, that is impossi-ble. His purpose is rather to bring persons to repentance, in the face of their incapacity to comply with the demands of His righteousness.

Although this option recognizes the seriousness of the de-mands of the Sermon on the Mount, it then proceeds to offer a theological way out of the difficulties which these demands create. In reality Jesus and His teachings are interpreted through the Pauline Epistles, and the writings of Paul, in turn, are read through the Constantinian glasses of Augustine and his successors in Western Christian history.

It is absolutely ridiculous to imagine that Jesus taught as He did in the Sermon on the Mount, and that the primitive church collected and preserved these teachings, merely to demonstrate that they are in reality an impossible ideal, and therefore, His followers will have to depend exclusively on grace for their salva-tion, as if this were possible apart from the righteousness of the kingdom.

### An interim ethic

Around the beginning of the twentieth century Johannes Weiss and Albert Schweitzer proposed this interpretation of the teachings of Jesus. They suggested that His teachings were valid for a very brief period preceding an expected catastrophic end of the world. According to them, Jesus expected an apocalyptic end within months, or at most, one or two years. Therefore we have in the Sermon on the Mount emergency measures to guide the heroic action of Jesus' followers until the apocalyptic irruption of the kingdom, which was imminent. This is why Jesus could afford to be so radical in His demands. He did not have to concern

Himself with the question of the survival of human social structures. When the imminent end failed to materialize, however, Christians did need to take responsibility for the preservation of social institutions.

In response to this it must be pointed out that there is no clear indication in the New Testament that this is what Jesus had in mind. Jesus was certainly not an ardent apocalyptist. His teachings do not appear to be the anxious expression of emergency measures in the face of an imminent catastrophic end. Quite to the contrary, the spirit which dominates the teachings of Jesus is His conviction that the kingdom of God and its salvation has appeared among humankind. The Sermon on the Mount describes some of the concrete forms in which this salvation expresses itself. Furthermore, to suppose that Jesus would have assumed responsibility for the survival of human social structures, in the event that the universe endured beyond His supposed expectations, implies assigning to these structures a value which Jesus was never willing to grant them.

### A futuristic ethic

Another variation of this interim ethic is found in the position taken by modern dispensationalism and has become popular through the version of the Bible edited by C. I. Scofield. In an attempt to understand the history of salvation, the saving activity of God as found in the Scriptures is divided into seven dispensations. It is held that Jesus proclaimed the gospel of the kingdom to the Jews and called on them to repent and enter the kingdom. However, in the face of their refusal, Jesus then offered, through the apostles and the Holy Spirit, salvation through grace to the Gentiles. Therefore, "the Sermon on the Mount, in its primary application, gives neither the privilege nor the duty of the church." °
The ethic described in the Sermon on the Mount is reserved for the dispensation of the future kingdom which will be initiated by the Parousia, or the second coming, of Jesus Christ. In this way

---

° *The Scofield Reference Bible*, edited by C. I. Scofield, p. 1000.

the full relevance of the Sermon on the Mount is limited to a period in the future.

But again, it is highly doubtful that this is what Jesus had in
mind when He gave these teachings. It is surely clear that the
early church did not understand its relevance in this way. In the
New Testament the kingdom is proclaimed to Gentiles as well as
Jews (Acts 28:28-31, *et al.*). The way in which the teachings of
Jesus found in the Sermon on the Mount are repeated in the New
Testament epistles makes one suppose that they were taken
seriously and held to apply to the early church. In fact the way in
which Matthew has gathered together Jesus' teachings in their
present form in the Sermon on the Mount seems to indicate that
the apostolic church used them in the instruction of new believer-
disciples.

## An ethic intended for a simple society

It is sometimes suggested that in order to understand Jesus'
teachings they must be viewed from the perspective of a rural or
pastoral setting—from the standpoint of a simple agrarian society
in which social relationships are direct and uncomplicated. After
all, Jesus had much to say about the birds of the air and the
flowers and grass which graced the Galilean countryside.
Therefore, the argument goes, the Sermon on the Mount was
relevant for the Galileans of the first century and could also be applied among the Franciscans of the Middle Ages and, by extension, to any group in any period which recreates the conditions of
a simple life by withdrawal from industrialized urban society, but
the teachings of Jesus are simply not applicable to the complexi-
ties of the highly urbanized situation of our times.

It is certainly true that there are marked differences between
first-century rural Palestine and the complex social structures of
the industrialized countries of the last quarter of the twentieth
century. But these are not the differences which would render
obsolete the teachings of Jesus. Jesus used images taken from nature as found in the Palestinian countryside in His teaching. But
He did this in order to warn men and women against being

anxious about material possessions. In fact Jesus speaks specifically to the problems which continue to concern people in the
twentieth century: how to treat offenders, the problem of violence, the question of money, the nature of authority and the
exercise of power, relationships between men and women, and
more. So we dare not arbitrarily assign to the teachings of Jesus a
value limited by temporal or cultural considerations.

The advocates of these ways of interpreting the Sermon on
the Mount represent a wide range of Christian viewpoints:
Catholic and Protestant, traditional denominations and groups of
recent origin, theological liberals and conservative funda-
mentalists, mainline Christians and "born-again evangelicals."
But in spite of their many differences, these groups all have in
common one thing—they interpret the Sermon on the Mount in a
way which confirms them in their own ethical practice. Even
those ethicists—like Reinhold Niebuhr—who do interpret the
ethical teachings of the Sermon on the Mount with literal seriousness fail to see it as the continuing norm for all Christians.

How should we interpret the Sermon on the Mount? Are
there keys which unlock its meaning? In the section that follows
we offer a series of suggestions which are found in the Sermon on
the Mount itself, which provide orientation for the interpretative
task.

### Questions for Discussion

1. According to the New Testament, was the Sermon on the
Mount for beginners in the messianic movement, or for a relative few
who wanted to be especially serious about their faith? How is it generally
thought of in your congregation?

2. Can you think of examples of ethical dualism other than the
ones cited in this chapter? What is the biblical alternative to this
dualism?

3. Do you feel that "salvation by faith" and "Sermon on the
Mount discipleship" are mutually exclusive? How can these two seemingly different approaches be harmonized? .

4. Is there any biblical evidence that Jesus intended the Sermon on
the Mount for some future golden age? Is there any evidence that it was
intended for guiding the life of the church?

5. Do you think that the Sermon on the Mount can be lived by Christians in industrialized Western society? What would be the implications of seriously attempting it?

6. Can you think of persons and communities who incorporate in their lives the values of the Sermon on the Mount? Would you say that they are "saved by faith" or do they depend on their "works" for their salvation?

7. Can you think of other ways, in addition to those mentioned in this chapter, in which the church has tried to assure its salvation independently of the values of the Sermon on the Mount?

# Chapter 3

# Internal Keys for Interpreting the Sermon on the Mount

The meaning of the words and phrases in which the teachings of the Sermon on the Mount are expressed are not generally questioned. They are sufficiently clear in their radical simplicity to be understood. Doubts do arise about whether these teachings offer ethical norms which are realistic, or possible to achieve, or relevant. Convinced as we are that the language of the Sermon on the Mount is essentially clear in its basic thrust, the focus of attention in this section will be limited to a series of observations on the way in which Jesus and His first listeners, the disciples, understood the Sermon on the Mount as well as the way in which Matthew understood it when he gathered together this block of Jesus' teachings in the form of a catechism for the basic instruction of new militants in the Jesus movement approximately one generation later.

### An ethic of repentance

As we have already pointed out, the chapters which precede the Sermon on the Mount in Matthew's Gospel indicate that a new era is dawning. In this context the initial message of Jesus takes on meaning, "Repent, for the kingdom of heaven is at hand." This invitation is fundamental for our understanding of the Sermon on the Mount. In order to prepare His disciples for the life of the new age which is dawning, Jesus describes a style of life which is breathtakingly new, which is without precedent in the history of fallen humankind, and which flows against the generally acceptable social current. It is an ethic of repentance. To live this new kind of social reality requires a radical reorientation of the will. The Sermon on the Mount does not offer to the world the bright new secret of happiness for which it is longing. It is not really a brilliant new program for social organization. The Sermon gives a simple and beautiful description of the ethic which characterizes that community of people who have been transformed by the Spirit of Jesus. Repentance means a radical return to God's intention for humanity. This life described in the Sermon on the Mount presupposes a baptism "with the Holy Spirit and with fire" (Matthew 3:11).

### An ethic for disciples of Jesus

Although Matthew mentions the presence of the multitudes (Matthew 5:1; 7:28), it is clear that the teachings of the Sermon on the Mount are directed to the disciples of Jesus. It is an ethic for disciples. And these disciples are motivated in their obedience, not by the goals which they hope to attain, but rather by their Lord whose life and Spirit they reflect. The disciples understood very well that the Sermon on the Mount was first and foremost a description of the life of Jesus, the Messiah, whom they were confessing as followers. The teachings of the Sermon on the Mount were only for those who had responded to Jesus' call to form a part of the community of His followers. (Of course the invitation to become disciples of the Messiah is in no way exclusive. It is extended to all humankind.)

The ethic of the Sermon on the Mount presupposes the grace of God which transforms people and incorporates them into His kingdom. The problems which arise when one attempts to govern a society guided by the principles of the Sermon on the Mount were not questions which demanded an immediate answer on the part of Jesus' followers. Effectiveness and social responsibility are

not really determinative of faithfulness in discipleship. It is rather
a question of obedience. They did not need to concern themselves
with the task of imposing a Sermon on the Mount style of life on
an entire society, or with trying to guide human history in the
right direction. It was rather simply the question of beginning to
live the life of the kingdom by the Spirit of Jesus. In reality, this
kingdom lifestyle is the only one which will finally prove to be
valid when human history comes to an end. Therefore the Sermon
on the Mount describes the lifestyle of the future as well as the
present. Although Jesus' disciples are called to live against the current in this "present evil age," they are, in reality, people of the
future.

### A communitarian ethic

The teachings of Jesus found in the Sermon on the Mount
presuppose the existence of a new messianic community gathered
around the person of the Messiah. Protestant interpretation has
generally approached the Sermon on the Mount from an individualistic ethical perspective. Instead of conceiving of a new
community whose social life is ordered by these principles, it
understands the Sermon on the Mount ethic as applying to individuals independently of the new social reality of the kingdom of
God. However, the Sermon on the Mount reflects a communitarian spirit. Prayer is communitarian (Matthew 6:9-15). The
teachings on material wealth and money presuppose economic
practices which are fraternal, or communitarian (Matthew 6:19-
34). The quality of this common life leads to testimony which is
collective (Matthew 5:14-16). Although modern English transla-
tions do not reflect this fact, since "you" can be either singular or
plural, the frequency with which pronouns in the second person
plural are employed is noteworthy. And even where the second
person singular form is used, it simply serves to make more direct
and more concrete the application of ethical practices which
characterize the community. To the degree in which we understand the essentially communitarian thrust of the Sermon on the
Mount we will be freed from the modern atomistic spirit which

interprets the teachings of Jesus in terms of heroic individualistic efforts in the face of an indifferent, and even hostile, society.

### An ethic of witness

Jesus says that the community which lives the blessedness of the Sermon on the Mount *is* salt and light (Matthew 5:14, 15). What the messianic community *is*, as well as what it *does* and *says*, communicates the love of God (Matthew 5:16). The ethical stance of this community communicates the true nature of God. The ethical norms which guide these disciples are not finally determined by the results they hope to obtain by their actions, nor by rules which must be obeyed, but rather by the way in which they communicate to the world the love of God, a God who loves even His enemies (Matthew 5:3, 9, 16, 44-48). For Jesus, as well as for His hearers, the fundamental question in ethical decisions is the need to reflect faithfully the true nature of God.

### An ethic of fulfillment

It is apparent that one of the purposes of Jesus in the Sermon on the Mount is to encourage a more complete fulfillment of the spirit and intention of the provisions of the covenant which God has made with Israel (Matthew 5:17). In other words, Jesus advocates the fulfillment of God's original creation intention for the life of His people. Six times in chapter 5 we find the formula repeated, "You have heard that it was said ... but I say to you" (5:21, 27, 31, 33, 38, 43), in order to encourage the fulfillment of the law at a higher level which is more nearly in line with God's true intention. In doing this Jesus does not come into conflict with the law itself, but rather with contemporary interpretations of the law which tended to bring it within reach of persons in general so that it could be more easily kept (Matthew 5:20).

Jesus resisted the temptation to distinguish between the absolute demands of the law of God, on one hand, and ethical standards derived from the law which were more realistic, on the other hand, as the scribes and Pharisees were accustomed to do. Jesus collided with another domesticating tendency in the interpretation of the law by His contemporaries when He emphasized the importance of the inner attitude of the heart. By reducing the law to external ethical codes the scribes were, in effect, trying to make its keeping more accessible to people in general. However, Jesus insisted on keeping the ideal of God's original intention before people. Therefore the inner motivations, as well as outward actions, matter.

The question is sometimes asked whether the Sermon on the Mount is really gospel, or if it might be law; is it a matter of grace, or a question of works of the law? But even to formulate the question in this way betrays an essential misunderstanding of the character of Jesus' teachings in the Sermon on the Mount, to say nothing of having missed the implications of the gospel of the kingdom. To state the question in this way is to introduce a concept which is foreign to the thought of Jesus.

The Sermon on the Mount is gospel, according to the New Testament meaning of the term. The gospel of the kingdom is the gospel of salvation. The righteousness of this kingdom is the form which salvation takes in the movement inaugurated by Jesus. This, in effect, is what Matthew tells us in his introduction in the Sermon on the Mount. "And he went about all Galilee, teaching in their synagogues and preaching the gospel of the kingdom . . ." (Matthew 4:23).

### An ethic of love

In the Sermon on the Mount Jesus proclaims an ethic of "perfect" love (Matthew 5:48). Among the examples which Jesus uses to teach this kind of love, three are drawn from the sphere of enmity in personal relationships. Jesus teaches that love is the essential trait which characterizes interpersonal relationships. Furthermore, the measure of this love is to be determined by the very nature of God Himself.

Jesus does not pretend that His followers will attain an absolute moral perfection in an abstract or philosophical sense. He simply insists that His followers be like God in one specific way: that they do not limit themselves to loving their friends (after all, publicans as well as pagans are capable of this kind of love), but that they love their enemies, as well (5:45-48; Luke 6:36). While the old covenant limited the vengeance which could be exacted— not more than *one* eye for an eye and *one* tooth in exchange for a tooth—in the messianic ethic proclaimed by Jesus the norm governing interpersonal relationships will be a concern for the redemption of the offending person, precisely because this is the way God acts.

### An ethic of excess

Jesus expected that His disciples would exceed normal human expectations in their ethical comportment (Matthew 5:46, 47). The question, "What more are you doing than others?" (5:47) underlines the fact that the morality which Jesus teaches is an ethic of excess. The disciples of Jesus dare not limit themselves to those actions which others are capable of doing, nor to the ethical alternatives which any given situation appears to offer. The love of God does not allow itself to be limited by the ethical options which naturally arise out of a given situation. The disciple of Jesus expects, by the power of God's Spirit, to surpass the ethical alternatives superficially present in a given situation and to exceed moral possibilities which are merely human. It is to be expected that the disciple of Jesus will find the resources to surpass the normal range of possibilities which an ethic based on natural law offers.

### An ethic of reconciliation

Finally, we discover another key to the interpretation of the Sermon on the Mount in Jesus' note of concern for the welfare of the "brother" (Matthew 5:22-24). Deeds as well as intentions are to be evaluated in terms of the welfare of our peers. It is impossible to worship God appropriately without being reconciled to each other. The ethic of Jesus is essentially an ethic of reconciliation. Instead of basing His prohibition of killing on the sacred character of the blood (Genesis 9), or on the absolute value of human life as such (as humanistic philosophy generally does),

Jesus' command is based on the nature of communion between one person and another as both the reflection and the measure of one's communion with God. To love another to the point of giving one's own life for the other is to love as God has loved us.

Far from being a code of laws which is applicable to society in general and which accepts the terms society dictates, the Sermon on the Mount is a description of life as it is lived in the kingdom which Jesus came to inaugurate. On the other hand, to pretend to be moving toward that kingdom, without taking seriously the Sermon on the Mount, is to deceive oneself in relation to the true nature of that kingdom. Understood in the context of the kingdom of God which invades human history in the person of Jesus the Messiah in all of its radical newness, the ethic of the Sermon on the Mount not only becomes a possibility, but is in reality the only appropriate testimony to the true nature of God and His kingdom that has already come in the person of His Messiah—and will on the last day come in all the fullness of His glory.

## Questions for Discussion

1. In what sense is the biblical concept of repentance necessary for understanding the Sermon on the Mount? What have been the results in the church of approaching the Sermon on the Mount independently of this radical vision of repentance?

2. In your opinion, does the fact that the Sermon on the Mount is for disciples of Jesus limit its long-range effectiveness in the deepest sense of the term?

3. How has the Sermon on the Mount generally been approached by Protestants—as individuals or collectively? What differences might a collective, or communitarian, approach make?

4. In what sense does the life described in the Sermon on the Mount communicate a gospel message?

5. Do you see similarities between the Ten Commandments and the Sermon on the Mount? What are the significant differences? What are the implications of these similarities and differences?

6. What are the implications of viewing the Sermon on the Mount as an "ethic of excess"? Can this be reasonably expected of Christians?

# Chapter 4

# The Values of the Kingdom (Matthew 5:1-20)

Although multitudes were attracted by the message they heard and the works of healing they saw Jesus perform, the meaning which Matthew 5:1b, 2 appears to convey indicates that the disciples of Jesus were the direct recipients of the teachings included in the Sermon on the Mount. In the NEB version of this text, this fact emerges even more clearly. As already noted, the teachings of the Sermon on the Mount are best understood as an ethic for disciples, i.e., citizens of the messianic community which is being inaugurated with the presence of the Messiah.

The literary form known as the "beatitude" was quite common in the ancient world. A brief review of the ways in which these statements that begin with the adjective "blessed" were used will help us to understand the beatitudes which appear in the Sermon on the Mount. In classic Greek literature this adjective, generally translated "blessed," was commonly reserved to describe the gods, or to refer to particular human felicity in the popular proverbs of the time. This second usage of the term also came to characterize Judaism in the time of Jesus. However, in the Hebrew Psalms, where the use of the term is quite common, this state of "beatitude" took on a meaning which was very different from that found among the Greeks. In the Psalms, blessedness is based in personal trust in God and in obedience to His precepts. The term was also used of God.

Matthew and Luke frequently employ beatitudes and the contexts in which these appear will help us to understand their meaning in the Gospels. (See Matthew 11:6 and Luke 7:23; Matthew 13:16 and Luke 10:23; Matthew 16:17; Matthew 24:46 and Luke 12:37, 38, 43; Luke 1:45; 11:27, 28; 14:14, 15.) In these beatitudes four fundamental elements stand out. (1) They describe, without exception, a blessedness which finds its source in the presence and activity of Jesus. In other words, they are Christocentric or messianic beatitudes. (2) This blessedness is essentially related to participation in an eschatological kingdom. It is a felicity which is already present and experienced, but its full and definitive flowering will occur in the future kingdom, fully come. (3) This blessedness is at one and the same time promised, announced, and communicated by Jesus to those who hear and obey in faith in spite of the hard realities of suffering and persecution in the present. In this sense, the beatitudes are paradoxical. (4) This blessedness is invested with a cosmic character. It is finally, not creation as such, but creation as it is restored in Christ (or the new creation) which constitutes the felicity of the disciples of Jesus.

In the life of the church these beatitudes have often been misunderstood. At times they have been interpreted in legalistic terms of duty and reward: being poor in spirit *in order to* participate in the kingdom of heaven, being meek *in order to* inherit the earth, being merciful *in order to* obtain mercy, and so on. The beatitudes do not constitute a list of activities which one can set oneself to do through a simple act of the will.

At other times the beatitudes have been conceived of as Christian virtues which are optional by their very nature. They are seen as "counsels of perfection" which some Christians will be capable of keeping, but which not everyone should attempt: a Christian may be meek because meekness is his special gift, or because he dedicates himself to meekness with an iron will; another Christian will be merciful, or a peacemaker, because it comes naturally, or because she sets herself to the task.

As if authentic discipleship expressed itself in terms such as these! As if disciples were in a position to discuss the terms of their discipleship with their Lord! No! The beatitudes, rather, describe the lifestyle and the values which characterize the kingdom. It is expected that *all* of the members of the messianic community will reflect *all* of these characteristics in their daily life which they live by the grace of God and in the power of His Holy Spirit which is poured out upon *all* of His sons and daughters in the messianic era. The beatitudes are, in reality, a moving declaration of God's grace.

Blessed are all of those who, by the grace of God, participate in the new life of the messianic kingdom which already anticipates the coming of the future kingdom in all of its fullness: a kingdom of good for all of those who begin to participate in the destiny which awaits God's children, a kingdom of good for those whose style of life reflects God's real intention for all of humanity, a kingdom of good for all of those who, because their lives prefigure creation made new in Christ, must suffer the violence of evil ones in this age.

Of course these beatitudes were, above all, incarnated in the person of Jesus Christ. It was abundantly evident to the apostolic community that all of these characteristics of the kingdom had been manifested in Jesus of Nazareth with radiant clarity. He who came announcing that the kingdom of God is a gift to the poor was, Himself, poor and humble of spirit. The apostles saw in Jesus the One "that though he was rich, yet for your sake he became poor, so that by his poverty you might become rich" (2 Corinthians 8:9). Jesus was uniquely "gentle and lowly in spirit," and it was in Him that the apostles found rest (Matthew 11:29). The righteousness which Jesus brought was the justice of the kingdom of God in which those who are lost find salvation and life. In the apostolic church it was clearly understood that the "cause of Christ" and the "cause of justice" were really one and the same thing (Matthew 5:10, 11). In the figure of Jesus, the early church recognized the merciful Messiah who healed the sick, who restored the sight of the blind, who offered hope to the outcasts, and who finally gave Himself as an "offering" (literally, "alms," or "acts of mercy") in behalf of the poor of the land (Matthew 9:27; 15:22; 20:30, 31). In Jesus, people noted a degree of personal integrity and authenticity which lent authority to His condemnation of hypocritical rituals which are powerless to purify a person (Matthew 23). The primitive community saw in Jesus the very personification of the messianic peace, the shalom of God. It was Jesus who uniquely brought peace to them (John 14:27). However, they came to understand that it was a peace which could only be established by means of the "Lamb's war" (Matthew 10:34; Revelation 12:11; 17:14).

But above all, the early church perceived in Jesus the supreme model of vicarious sacrificial suffering. For that reason the cross became the clearest symbol for the opposition offered by the powers of this present evil age, and came to be central in the church's understanding of the saving work of Jesus Christ. The blessedness of vicarious suffering in behalf of the poor, the brokenhearted, the captives, the blind and the oppressed, envisioned in the suffering servant songs of Isaiah, has found its fullest realization in the person of Jesus. That is why the apostles pointed to Jesus as the model to be followed in suffering (1Peter 2:21-24).

Rather than presenting an idealistic, and somewhat utopian, vision for human society, the beatitudes describe realistically a concrete human person, Jesus of Nazareth. And not only Jesus, they also describe the messianic community, made up in the first century of the followers of Jesus who responded in faith and obedience to His gracious call.

### The Beatitudes (Matthew 5:3-12).

"*Blessed are the poor in spirit, for theirs is the kingdom of heaven*" (3). In the Lukan version of this beatitude we read, "Blessed are you poor, for yours is the kingdom of God" (6:20). There are evident differences in the two versions. However, the difference between "poor in spirit" and "poor" in the two versions is probably not substantial. Matthew's version is more prone to the loss of its radicality in the hands of some of its interpreters. However, this is undoubtedly due more to the spiritualizing tendencies of the interpreters than to the real meaning of the Matthean wording, "poor in spirit" (i.e., spirit of poorness). In Matthew, Jesus was surely not referring to those who, in spite of the fact that they are rich, try to live spiritually unattached to their riches. According to Jesus, the poor are blessed. And the "spirit of poorness" is essential for entrance into the kingdom of heaven.

The pronouns "you" and "yours" in the Lukan version simply underline the meaning of "theirs" in Matthew's Gospel. These emphatic pronouns point to a specific community, to the messianic community, in contrast to Judaism in general. In other words, we should remember that the beatitudes describe the life of the community of the Messiah in contrast to all other human societies.

We dare not underestimate the fundamental importance of the first beatitude for our understanding of the gospel of the kingdom. It points to a basic characteristic of the Messiah Himself, as well as of the kingdom which He brings. In a sense, all of the rest of the beatitudes are already contained in this one. No one can enter the kingdom of God as a rich person. The kingdom is entered by those who come as poor persons (Mark 10:21). The kingdom is composed by those characterized by their spirit of poorness, by those who choose to be poor. According to Jesus those who choose to be last will, in reality, be first (Mark 10:31). To be poor is to renounce all ambition to possess wealth and power. It means not considering wealth as an autonomous value (Matthew 6:19-21). It means opting in favor of God, and against money, as Lord of our life (Matthew 6:24). The disciple of Jesus is willing to renounce the security which wealth promises and to deposit his confidence in God (Mark 10:21).

In Hebrew thought the poor man refers typically to the humble person. These are the ones who, in their seemingly endless experience of social and economic misery, have learned to trust in God alone for their salvation. The Hebrew mind accentuates more the modest and humble condition of the poor than the actual absence of the necessities of life. The arrogance and self-assurance which are so characteristic of the rich are not real temptations to the poor. The Old Testament abounds in references to the poor as they were understood in ancient Hebrew society (Psalms 34:6; 37:14; Isaiah 61:1; cf. Luke 4:18; 7:22; Matthew 11:5; Isaiah 66:2; Zephaniah 2:3). In the messianic vision of Isaiah which we find reflected in the Servant Songs, it is precisely those who are poor and oppressed who are the recipients of the good news brought by the Messiah.

The opposite of this "spirit of poorness" is a spirit of pride. It is pride which leads a person to hold an exaggerated view of supposed self-importance. It is the "poor in spirit" who is freed from these false and distorted self-images in order to reflect the true intention of God for life in His restored creation.

Of course, the supreme model of this "spirit of poorness" is Jesus Christ who for our sake "became poor" (2 Corinthians 8:9) and "humbled himself" (Philippians 2:8). Followers of Jesus are the ones who choose to be poor in a world which is oriented in the opposite direction. The truly humble person views reality from the best perspective, the perspective of the kingdom, "for theirs *is* the kingdom of heaven." This is the spirit which characterizes the citizens of the kingdom which Jesus came to inaugurate.

There is in Western Christianity a widely held understanding which views the gospel as an instrument which promotes upward social and economic mobility. The gospel which is preached to the poor will most certainly lead to prosperity, it is claimed. But this view, which is so common among evangelical Christians, can easily become a shamefully twisted version of the gospel of Jesus Christ. In reality the social and economic mobility to which Jesus calls us is toward the poor (Romans 12:16). The gospel is a call to orient our lives according to the Spirit of Jesus Himself who "emptied himself taking the form of a servant" (Philippians 2:5-8).

Of course, there have been some, during the history of the Christian church, who have tended to glorify poverty as a value in and of itself. Jesus expects among His disciples attitudes of detachment and generosity in relation to material wealth. Material goods should be used in the service of humanity, rather than being allowed to exercise dominion over self. The children of the kingdom will work in productive occupations, just as other persons do, but instead of being motivated by the desire to enrich themselves personally, they will work in order to contribute to the welfare of their comrades (Ephesians 4:28).

*"Blessed are those who mourn, for they shall be comforted"* (4). This beatitude, as well as the ones which follow, does not designate a new category of persons, but rather describes more fully those who have already been identified as poor or humble. All of the beatitudes describe that new messianic community of believer-disciples which forms around Jesus. "Those who mourn," in its grammatical form in the Greek text (present participle), describe the character, or the essential nature of these disciples. They are persons who are deeply troubled. They are not melancholic people or chronic criers, but rather they are persons who are saddened and deeply concerned. These are those who are "waiting for the consolation of Israel." A considerable part of their affliction arises out of their concern for the welfare of persons around them. They weep over the evil which befalls their people due to the general indisposition to repent and find authentic beatitude within the community of the Messiah.

Authentic repentance, which is a requirement for entrance into the kingdom, involves a radical reorientation toward life and a transformation of values that place one in direct conflict with the scale of values which characterizes life in a fallen world. This fundamental opposition of values and lifestyle will undoubtedly bring about affliction which is both subjective (deep concern for others) and objective (the pain which results from persecution). These are people who do not feel good about things as they are in the world. They are not happy with the prevailing value system nor with the forms which human relations generally take in society. But it is not merely a question of subjective suffering that occurs within the spirit of the disciple. It is also objective and concrete suffering which comes as a result of the opposition and persecution inflicted by a world that is oriented by a system of values which is altogether different.

The Servant of Yahweh, according to the vision of Isaiah, would come to "bring good tidings to the afflicted ... to bind up the brokenhearted ... to comfort all who mourn; to grant to those who mourn in Zion a garland instead of ashes, the oil of gladness instead of mourning, the mantle of praise instead of a faint spirit" (Isaiah 61:1—3). This is precisely the consolation of Israel for which the poor and the humble of the New Testament hoped and waited (Luke 2:25). And this is the consolation which is experienced in the kingdom that has come in the person and ministry of Jesus.

Only those who are uncomfortable with the system of values which characterizes the present age, those who through deep and painful repentance have radically changed their values and lifestyles, only these will be in a position to experience the authentic consolation of the messianic kingdom. To these belongs the true joy of their Lord.

*"Blessed are the meek, for they shall inherit the earth"* (5). This beatitude appears to be a direct allusion to Psalm 37:11. The context within which this phrase is set in the psalm will help us to understand its meaning here in the Sermon on the Mount. The meek person is nonviolent, trusting in God, placing hope in Him. The meek one is just and merciful. Poor and humble, the meek one has no other alternative than to depend upon the Lord for survival. In Psalm 37 this is the person who is contrasted with the wicked, the wrongdoers, the one who carries out evil devices, who plots against the righteous, who brings down the poor and the needy, the violent one who slays those who walk uprightly. The meek person, then, is characterized by concern for justice and peace and whose survival ultimately depends upon a God who is just and loving.

The meek person, therefore, is not a dispirited and timid individual. A truly meek person in poorness and humility submits self fully in dependence on God. Moses is the classic biblical example of meekness, a virtue which for him took forty years in the desert to learn. In his youth Moses had been a typical revolutionary. In the face of the injustices which his people were suffering at the hands of the Egyptians he took the cause of justice into his own hands and violently avenged the unjust death of his Hebrew brother. But finally, after long years in the desert, Moses learned to await a word from God and to submit himself under the lordship of Yahweh. True meekness is the product of confidence and faith in God.

Matthew employs the term "meek" two more times in his Gospel. And both times he uses the expression to describe the character of Jesus. In Matthew 11:29 Jesus is described as being "gentle [the Greek text has "meek"] and lowly in heart," and inviting all who labor and are heavy-laden to find rest in Him. In Matthew 21:5 Jesus is described in the words of the prophet, "Behold your king is coming to you, humble [here again the Greek text has "meek"] and mounted on an ass." In this text meekness clearly has to do with the absence of violence. Matthew uses this figure to present Jesus as a nonviolent King. Matthew gives us to understand that meekness is an essential characteristic of the Messiah, as well as of His disciples who participate in the messianic community.

In Psalm 37 it was the promised land which God would graciously give to the meek and the humble. In the Sermon on the Mount Jesus offers the "promised land" of the kingdom to the meek and humble. In his Gospel, Luke describes how the kingdom will be given through the gracious action of God to His people. "Instead, seek his kingdom, and these things shall be yours as well. Fear not, little flock, for it is your Father's good pleasure to give you the kingdom" (Luke 12:31, 32).

According to the biblical vision, the true meaning of history flows through the channel of the kingdom of God. When human history reaches its end, the meek of God, together with their meek and humble Lord, will prevail rather than violent and self-seeking men. We should not be deceived. Those who appear to be great and powerful upon the earth will not have the last word, in spite of all the indications to the contrary. At the end of time it will be the Lamb who has been slain who is "worthy . . . to receive power and wealth and wisdom and might and honor and glory and blessing" (Revelation 5:6, 12).

In their meekness the citizens of the kingdom which Jesus came to establish are simply prefiguring the conditions that will prevail when that kingdom comes in all of its fullness and their Lord is manifested as "the Lamb that was slain," as meek and lowly. This patient confidence in the One who will be the vindicator of the humiliated is very much different from the attitude of the Zealots which led them to wage guerrilla warfare, and of the Essenes of Qumran, who predicted the coming of a holy war in which they would be participants. The triumphant confidence of the meek is also very different from the spirit of servility and abject subjection which sometimes seem to characterize oppressed peoples who live without any real hope of salvation. For their part, the meek of the messianic community are those who dare to live in hope.

Of course, this understanding of the essential blessedness of the meek is too revolutionary to have been accepted by the Christian church in the course of its history. If we were really capable of capturing this vision of the blessedness of the meek, our very being would be radically changed. It would make a fundamental difference in our scale of values, in our style of life, in our social and economic relationships, and (why not say it) in almost all of our life and activity in the church.

*"Blessed are those who hunger and thirst for righteousness, for they shall be satisfied"* (6). This is a graphic way of describing the ardent desire and the urgent necessity which kingdom citizens feel for justice. The people who suffer hunger, and above all, thirst, are those who find themselves at the very limits of their resistance (cf. Psalms 42:2, 3; Amos 8:11). This is an expression of the depth of desire to witness and experience those right social relationships which characterize the messianic kingdom. Although, in his version, Luke does not add the word "righteous-

ness" ("Blessed are you that hunger now, for you shall be satisfied" [6:21]), surely his variant of the beatitude should be understood in the same sense it is given in Matthew. After all, the blessings of the messianic kingdom are not limited to bread (although they most certainly include it). They, rather, take in the entire range of right and just social relationships which characterize "righteousness" in Hebrew thought. The prophetic understanding of righteousness, or justice, is practically synonymous with the terms peace and salvation (Isaiah 51:5-8; 52:7). It includes that wide range of virtues which contributes to relationships among persons, and between persons and God, which are right and whole (healed). In short, righteousness describes the quality of relationships which characterizes life together in the kingdom. In the Gospel of Matthew righteousness often means a good relationship with God which is attained by means of submission to His will. In the context of the Sermon on the Mount it is transparently clear that God's will implies ordering one's life according to the values embodied in Jesus' teachings. So in reality, righteousness has to do with relationships among persons, as well as between God and people.

This righteousness was surely different from the kind of moralism which characterized the scribes and Pharisees of Jesus' time (Matthew 5:20). Justice, in Hebrew thought, was a broad concept of right interpersonal relationships which were harmonious, as well as just. It included human well-being in its broadest sense. It had to do with a life characterized by love, that is, the disposition to live in behalf of one's fellow human beings. This beatitude describes the person whose deepest drives and desires are directed toward the well-being of others: their welfare, their peace, their salvation, in short, true justice.

The kingdom of God is a kingdom of "righteousness and peace and joy in the Holy Spirit" (Romans 14:17). Therefore those who "hunger and thirst for righteousness" will surely be satisfied in this kingdom. While it is true that they will be ultimately satisfied in the fulfillment of the kingdom at the end of time, meanwhile, the place where this hunger and thirst for righteousness will be most fully satisfied is in the messianic kingdom which is characterized by justice.

*"Blessed are the merciful, for they shall obtain mercy"* (7). Judging from the way in which Matthew uses the term in his Gospel, to be merciful means to pardon the offenses of others (9:13; 12:7; 18:33; 23:23), as well as to do good to all who are needy, be they the two blind men who asked to have their sight restored (9:27; 20:30, 31), or the demon-possessed daughter of the Canaanite woman (15:22). Therefore, citizens of the messianic kingdom are characterized both by their readiness to forgive the sins of others, as well as by their willingness to contribute to the well-being of anyone who may be in need.

The messianic kingdom is the community in which forgiveness is experienced, where the forgiveness of God becomes a reality which is communicated through brothers and sisters within His family (Matthew 18:15-20). The meaning of this beatitude is perfectly illustrated in the parable of the unmerciful servant (Matthew 18:21-35). Although the future form of the verb "shall obtain" which is used in the beatitude can refer to the ultimate mercy of God, it is not limited to this, because the messianic community, or the church, is precisely the sphere in which the mercy of God assumes a concrete form in the forgiveness and restoration of the erring brother or sister. There is a very close relationship between being merciful and obtaining mercy, between forgiving and experiencing forgiveness. This condition upon which forgiveness seems to be based is repeated no less than six times in the New Testament (Matthew 6:12; 6:14, 15; 18:35; Mark 11:25; Ephesians 4:32; Colossians 3:13). In addition to the forgiveness of sins which is experienced in the messianic community, other works of mercy also flourish. These expressions of mercy contribute to the healing, the well-being, and the salvation of brothers and sisters in the family of God.

*"Blessed are the pure in heart, for they shall see God"* (8). In ancient Jewish thought "heart" and "spirit" are used inter-

changeably to refer to the inner springs of moral responsibility within a person. This beatitude describes a person who is sincere, whose loyalty is undivided, whose morality is marked by integrity. To serve God and one's fellowmen with "all one's heart" is to serve without feigned piety and calculating self-interest. The man described in Psalm 24:4 is a good example of the virtue described in this beatitude—"He who has clean hands and a pure heart, who does not lift up his soul to what is false, and does not swear deceitfully." It refers to sincerity, to transparency of intention and character, to purity of purpose.

In the New Testament purity of heart is contrasted with external ritual purity which is obtained through certain ceremonial practices. This was a frequent subject of controversy between Jesus and the Pharisees. Matthew 15:10-20 explains something of what Jesus understood purity of heart to be: that fundamental personal integrity which expresses itself in words and deeds of compassionate concern.

This integrity which characterizes the people of God stands in sharp contrast to the hypocrisy which Jesus condemned among the Jews of His time. A hypocrite was originally an actor in the theatrical productions of ancient Greece who wore a mask in the presentation of his role. Participation in the kingdom which Jesus came to inaugurate requires authentic repentance which permits us to be sincere and open before God, of course, but also in the presence of our brothers and sisters. A person who is not sincere with his peers will scarcely be sincere with God, nor with self.

In Psalm 11:7 it is the upright person who will behold God's face, because "the Lord is righteous, [and] he loves righteous deeds." To behold the face of God in the kingdom which Jesus came to inaugurate requires uprightness, sincerity, and integrity which spring forth from a heart which has been truly transformed. To see God in the messianic community is the preamble to that blessed vision which will be ours when the kingdom comes in all of its fullness and glory (Revelation 22:3, 4).

*"Blessed are the peacemakers, for they shall be called sons of*

*God"* (9). Among all of the beatitudes, this one has probably been most misunderstood by the Christian church throughout its history. Perhaps the Latin Vulgate translation, "beati pacifici," has unwittingly contributed to this misunderstanding. In reality, "pacifici" are peacemakers, which reproduces quite well the original Greek term that means "doers of peace." However, in the subsequent life of the church this beatitude has come to be understood in terms of peaceful persons, of those who are pacific, or at best, pacifiers. This, of course, is a far cry from the "creators of shalom" which Jesus had in mind. This marked mutation of meaning which the term has undergone was possible only because the Christian church moved away from its roots in historic Judaism and took on Greek and Roman meanings of peace. We do well to remember that, by definition, the peacemaker is an activist. He is a creator of peace. He, like God, loves his enemies, making peace and reconciliation, rather than destruction, live possibilities. Peacemakers are those who contribute joyfully and hopefully to the full manifestation of that peace, justice, and salvation which characterizes the coming of the messianic kingdom.

Peace in this beatitude should be understood in its biblical Hebrew meaning, shalom. We should remember that Jesus and His disciples were Jews in their ways of thinking and doing. Shalom was a fundamental concept among the Hebrew people. It meant well-being, or health, or salvation in its fullest sense, material as well as spiritual. It described the situation of well-being which resulted from authentically whole (healed) relationships among persons, as well as between persons and God. According to the Old Testament prophets, shalom reigned in Israel when there was social justice, when the cause of the poor and the weak was vindicated, when there was equal opportunity for all, in short, when the people enjoyed salvation according to the intention of God expressed in His covenant. On the other hand, when there were injustices, when there was suffering caused by social and economic oppression, there was no shalom.

Jeremiah denounced the levity with which the false prophets of his time cried "peace, peace" (6:14). In reality, he declared, "there is no peace" because there is no justice, the rights of the needy are not defended, and because the rich and powerful deal deceitfully with the weak and the vulnerable (Jeremiah 5:25-29). Among the ancient Hebrews, peace was not merely the absence of armed conflict, but rather the prevalence of conditions which contribute to the genuine well-being of the people in all of their social and spiritual relationships. Hebrew shalom was not merely a matter of tranquility of spirit nor serenity of mind. It was a matter of harmonious relationships between God and His people, and righteousness and concord among all the people. In reality the terms peace, justice, and salvation are practically synonymous and describe the well-being that results when persons live together in the harmony created by relationships which are right and just. This peace is a gift of God to His people.

In Acts 10:36 God is pictured as taking the initiative in sending His message to Israel, "preaching good news of peace by Jesus Christ." Colossians 1:19, 20 presents God reconciling to Himself all things through Jesus His Messiah, "making peace by the blood of his cross." In Ephesians 2:14-16 the essential work of Jesus Christ is the creation of the new humanity. Peoples who were enemies of one another and alienated from God are reconciled, "so making peace." In this context reconciliation means concretely overcoming the causes of enmity which kept the Jews and the Gentiles separated. So in reality, peacemakers who dedicate themselves to the creation of God's shalom are participants in God's mission in the world. Peacemakers bear a very special relationship with the "God of Peace." This is why "they shall be called the sons of God." Among other things, this undoubtedly means that at the final judgment God will declare that they are His sons (Revelation 21:7). But even more, in the kingdom which has been inaugurated in Jesus, peacemakers will be recognized for what they already are: sons of God. In the Old Testament this is one of the titles which was applied to Israel. Those who heal the causes of discord and injustice show that they are members of the true Israel of God.

Among the ancient Hebrews, the expression "son of" was

also used to describe the character of a person. James and John were called "the sons of thunder," in all probability, because of their hot temper and their volatile nature (Mark 3:17). Barnabas was called "the son of encouragement" for obvious reasons, no doubt (Acts 4:36). "Sons of wrath," in addition to being irascible persons, were those whose actions and attitudes placed them under the judgment of God. Those who, in the kingdom, struggle to create the conditions of true shalom, reconciling alienated persons among themselves and with God are, in reality, participating in the mission of God Himself. God is the peacemaker *par excellence* who creates His shalom among people, doing good to all peoples equally, loving even His enemies. "Sons of God" are those who are like God in their peacemaking.

Rather than merely being peaceful or serene persons, peacemakers are in reality God's activists engaged in the task of healing in the midst of a broken world.

*"Blessed are those who are persecuted for righteousness' sake, for theirs is the kingdom of heaven"* (10). The last two beatitudes (which should probably be considered as one, since verses 11 and 12 simply develop the theme already stated in verse 10) point to the fact that the disciples of Jesus, who are described in the first seven beatitudes, are also persecuted. The grammatical form of the verb translated "are persecuted" (perfect tense) indicates that this persecution is the result of a prior situation. It is implied here that it is the kind of life which characterizes the messianic community described in the first seven beatitudes which evokes the world's violence and brings on persecution.

"For theirs *is* [present tense] the kingdom of heaven." Citizens of the kingdom which has come in Jesus suffer persecution at the hands of the world because their radically different scale of values renders them intolerable. In reality, the persecution that kingdom citizens receive at the hands of the world gives testimony to the fact that the values which characterize Jesus' disciples are inspired by a different Spirit. In fact, the object pronouns in verses 11 and 12 occur in the second person *plural,* "you" (a fact which escapes the readers of most English versions). This means that they are directed to the entire messianic community made up of disciples of Jesus. While it is true that the cross was the verdict which the world pronounced upon the life and work of Jesus, it is also true that the reviling and the persecutions which the Jesus community suffers are the world's verdict on the kingdom values which characterize the movement. In the messianic community this reviling is borne with joy because it simply serves to identify the members as true disciples of Jesus (1 Peter 4:13, 14).

Unbound joy and happiness characterize the citizens of the kingdom. In addition to understanding persecution as an involuntary testimony that their life does in fact correspond to the kingdom, they look forward to the rewards of this righteousness. The term translated "reward" (12) can also be translated recompense or payment. (The same term is employed in Matthew 6:1). The life of genuine good fortune described in the Sermon on the Mount amounts to the shalom of God, to authentic well-being, to salvation, not only within the limits of human history, but also in the final and full realization of the kingdom. It is not a question of doing the righteousness which corresponds to the messianic community in order to receive the reward. It is, rather, a matter of participating by the grace of God and authentic repentance in the blessedness of kingdom living which, by its very nature, leads to the beatitude of the kingdom fully come.

"For so men persecuted the prophets who were before you" (12) is a phrase which serves to remind those who are persecuted that their sufferings are neither new, nor accidental, nor absurd. They are charged with significance when viewed from the perspective of the history of salvation. A glance at the history of God's people shows that His true witnesses have always suffered at the hands of evil persons. The disciples of Jesus should not be surprised when this happens (1 Peter 4:12). Jesus and His followers are the true successors of the prophets (Matthew 10:41; 13:17; 23:34). Therefore the followers of Jesus should expect to receive the same verdict from the world in response to their life and work as the one handed down in the case of the true prophets of an earlier period.

### Salt and light (Matthew 5:13-16)

The essential relationship between this paragraph and the preceding one is highlighted by the use of the plural pronoun "you," first in verses 11 and 12, and now in verses 13 and 14. In the Greek text "you" is given special emphasis, both by the grammatical form which the pronoun takes and by the position it occupies in the sentence. It is as if Jesus had said: "*You*, as hearers of my words and participants in my kingdom, *you* are therefore persecuted. It is precisely *you* who are the salt of the earth and the light of the world."

It is not by accident that in the New Testament the same term applies to both martyr and witness. Suffering and testimony are two sides of the same coin in the messianic community. It is this suffering community gathered around a suffering Messiah which will be salt in the earth and light in the world through the character of its life and works that correspond to the kingdom which Jesus has brought. These are precisely the characteristics that we find further described in the Sermon on the Mount. As it lives according to these teachings of Jesus, his community will show forth the loving kindness of their "Father who is in heaven" and He will be glorified by all who perceive.

It is noteworthy that the principle verbs in verses 13 and 14 are in the indicative mood rather than in the imperative—a fact which is often inadvertently overlooked in the interpretation of these verses. Jesus does not command His disciples to be salt and light. If we are, by the grace of God, the kind of people whom Jesus describes in the beatitudes and if, in the power of His spirit, we do good works, such as the ones which will be described in the rest of the Sermon on the Mount, then our presence will serve to season and purify and enlighten interpersonal relationships within human society in which we are immersed. However, if we are not the kind of persons described in the beatitudes and if our works do not correspond to the teachings of Jesus which follow, then no matter how hard we may try, we will lose our saltiness and we will become insipid and worthless.

In His use of the image of light, Jesus underscores the missionary visibility of the people of God. The community described in the beatitudes and whose works correspond to those of the Messiah will be light for the world. In addition to the missionary dimensions found in the quality of life that characterizes the citizens of the kingdom, verses 14-16 point to the importance of the visibility of these works which correspond to the messianic community. "A city set on a hill cannot be hid ... it gives light to all in the house ... let your light so shine before all men" (14, 15) are all phrases which underline the importance of a witness of presence and works in the midst of human society. One is tempted to ask if Jesus was not responding to the strategy of the Essenes who withdrew to the Judean desert and there lived together in communities which in some ways might be considered as ideal. There they dedicated themselves to living lives of purity, both moral and religious, while they awaited an apocalyptic intervention by God and the final establishment of His kingdom. In marked contrast, Jesus tells His disciples that they are to live out the life of the new era in a very visible form in the midst of human society. They are expected to realize already in this present time, the values of the kingdom which will finally come in all its fullness at the end of history. In this sense Jesus expects that His disciples will live the life of the kingdom in an anticipatory way. The image of the city in verse 14 speaks of the city of God which will one day "come down out of heaven" (Revelation 21:2), but which has already been inaugurated in the person of the Messiah. In both cases the Lord Himself who abides in its midst is its source of light (John 8:12; Revelation 21:23).

As a result of this highly visible testimony, which includes the entire life and activity of the messianic community in the midst of human society, it is expected that God will be glorified. To glorify God, in biblical thought, is to recognize Him as the only true God. The Jews could not conceive of the knowledge of God prior to, or independent of, His glorification. To glorify God is to know Him in truth. This glorification of the God of Israel by all peoples and nations was one of the clearest characteristics of the messianic era according to Jewish expectations. So the life and works which correspond to the messianic community are the clearest testimony that God has truly intervened in human history and that His reign has begun in an anticipatory way.

The vital presence of the kingdom community in the midst of human society will contribute to its transformation, not by means of coercion nor through revolutionary violence, but by the penetrating and efficacious power of love. The very best contribution which the people of God can make to society is that of lives and works which already participate in the "age to come" and which point toward the quality of relationships which characterize the kingdom of God. By being and doing, the messianic community becomes an instrument of the saving action of God.

The idea that only two alternatives are open to the people of God—(1) conform to the values which characterize society in general, or (2) maintain a different style of life by withdrawing from the world and living in geographic or spiritual isolation—is false. The option which Jesus invites His disciples to take is to live and work in a radically different way, experiencing the life of the kingdom in the midst of the world.

This kind of testimony will most surely awaken one of the following responses among those who receive it. 1) They will perceive the love and kindness of God through the life of His people and will glorify Him. 2) They will be threatened by the way in which the style of life which corresponds to the age to come judges the values which determine life in this present evil age and will resist this intrusion by means of violence and persecution. 3) And many, where the radical implications of the message of the kingdom have not been communicated with clarity, will simply remain indifferent.

### Jesus and the Law (Matthew 5:17-20)
The observations included in this paragraph about the function of law in the messianic era have probably been included by

Matthew in order to correct some sort of misunderstanding. It is noteworthy that the term translated "think" in verse 17 is also used in this sense in Matthew 10:34 and Matthew 20:10.

Jesus rejected the idea that the messianic mission which He had received from God was to lead people away from the authentic and legitimate authority of the law of God over them. On the contrary, He had been commissioned by God to "give fullness" to the "law and the prophets," an expression which was used to designate the Scriptures as a unit. Jesus sets His teachings in the context of law. As Messiah, Jesus is the new Moses, lawgiver *par excellence*. As a Jew, and as the Messiah, the category of law was not alien to Jesus. For those who have inherited the Protestant tradition, law and gospel are generally viewed as antithetical categories. However, for Jesus the category of law was as native and congenial as the gospel of the kingdom which He proclaimed. As Messiah, Jesus understood God's law as the expression of His highest intention for the life of His people. Therefore Jesus offers His teachings as the culmination, as the full flowering, of the intention of God expressed in the Scriptures. Jesus comes as One who carries the law of God to its completion, to all the fullness of God's intention.

In the six examples which follow (Matthew 5:21-48) the purpose of Jesus in relation to the law is made clear. In reality, Jesus radicalizes the law, that is, He gives it its fullest meaning in the direction of the essential intention of God for humankind. Taking as His point of departure its root (Latin—radix from which radical is derived) in the intention of God, Jesus in each case, carries law to its fullest expression in the purpose of God for His people.

Jesus radicalizes the prohibition of killing (5:21) with a more far-reaching prohibition of all forms of anger and lack of sincere respect for the integrity of the brother. In this, Jesus gives God's commandment fuller meaning in the direction of His original intention.

In the same way, the prohibition which forbids adultery (5:27) is carried forward to its fullest expression in which lustful desire and the intention of sexual infidelity which would destroy the conjugal harmony of others are forbidden.

According to the intention of Mosaic law, a certificate of divorce served to protect the rights of the wife who had been repudiated by her husband (5:31). But Jesus radicalizes this commandment by basing His teaching on the original intention of God Himself, expressed in creation, by forbidding divorce (Matthew 19:4-6; Mark 10:2-12; Genesis 1:27).

While the oath (5:33) served to maintain a certain degree of public honesty among the ancient Hebrews, Jesus carries this commandment forward to its fullest expression of the intention of God by requiring veracity and sincerity in all interpersonal relationships, rendering the oath unnecessary.

The measure of "an eye for an eye and a tooth for a tooth" (5:38) was not the law of the jungle, but rather a truly humanitarian measure. The "law of talion" served, in reality, to limit the degree of retaliation. It permitted only *one* eye for an eye, and not more than *one* tooth for a tooth. But Jesus also carried this provision forward to the fullest expression of the will of God—a genuinely redemptive concern for the person who does evil.

And finally, the understanding of the love of one's neighbor is taken radically by Jesus over against the tradition of the Qumran community, for example, which allowed and even demanded, hatred of outsiders. Jesus radically extended this commandment to love the neighbor (5:43) to include love for the enemy, a provision which responds more fully to the very nature of God Himself.

So Jesus deepens the understanding of law which was commonly held by His contemporaries, discerning its essential spirit and its radical intention. Then He gives a new prescription which fully expresses the intention of God and carries it forward to a new level in full accord with the divine will. It is precisely in this that Jesus fulfills His messianic function. As a part of their messianic expectation, the Jews looked forward to the last times when there would be an authoritative and definitive interpretation of the law of God (Jeremiah 31:31 ff.; Isaiah 2:3; 59:21; Ezekiel 36:26, 27). In reality, in the person of Jesus of Nazareth humanity is confronted by the clearest and the fullest revelation of the intention of God.

Jesus' respect for the law of God is expressed in terms of the value of the very smallest of the elements used in its transcription (5:18).

In the relationship between "doing" and "teaching" (19) the commandments should be understood from the perspective of Jewish thought. According to this tradition doing and teaching form an indissoluble unity. One must personally submit oneself to the law of God and, doing so, must teach others to submit themselves to the law. In reality, this is precisely what Jesus has done in His relation to the law. As Messiah, He "learned obedience" (Hebrews 5:8) and taught "as one who had authority" (Matthew 7:29). The words "least" and "great" in verse 19 should not be understood as expressions of hierarchy in the kingdom. They should probably be understood as Jewish expressions for exclusion from, or participation in, the kingdom.

For Jesus, the gospel does not imply living independently of the law in contrast to a life lived under the law of the old dispensation. The contrast is rather between law, as it was observed by Jesus' contemporaries, the scribes and Pharisees, on one hand, and the law as the expression of the intention of God for humankind carried to its fullness in His messianic mission. This is the "law of Christ" to which Paul refers (1 Corinthians 9:21; Galatians 6:2). Instead of the law as understood by the scribes and Pharisees, Jesus offers His own yoke (Matthew 11:29, 30). Therefore the law which the disciples of Jesus are to practice and to teach is the law completed and fulfilled in the Messiah. By keeping the law, and the traditions which had grown up around it, it was possible to produce a righteousness similar to that of the scribes and the Pharisees, but in no case was this righteousness sufficient to gain entrance into the kingdom of heaven (5:20). The righteousness which Jesus expects of His disciples calls for submission to the will of God as it has been fully made known in His own person.

The well-known aphorism of Augustine, "Love and do what you will," has sometimes been commended by Christians as a rule of thumb for making moral decisions. It is possible that this saying is not always understood in the sense that Augustine intended. In fact, it has probably been twisted on occasions to fit the desires of people looking for an easy way out of difficult ethical decisions. Therefore when this key is interpreted in the sense that love is capable of creating its own law independently of the specific ethical teachings of Jesus, it becomes a dangerous tool for softening the radicality of Jesus' teachings.

As Jesus well knew, love alone, even that of his disciples, is an inadequate criteria for making ethical decisions. Love, in and of itself, is incapable of supplying the substance of our moral comportment in the world. Love furnishes a safe basis for making ethical decisions only inasmuch as Jesus is concretely the definition of that love. Jesus, in His spirit and His words and His deeds, as He is presented in the New Testament and with special clarity, in the Sermon on the Mount, provides the specific content for the moral performance of Christians. Therefore, far from being characterized by an absence of law, the life of the messianic community is lived under the law of God carried to its highest expression in the person of the Messiah. This is the new life of faith lived by the grace of God and in the power of His Holy Spirit which partakes of the very nature of the kingdom of heaven.

*Questions for Discussion*

1. Do you feel that *all* of the beatitudes can be expected to describe *all* members of the messianic community? Why?

2. What does it mean to be characterized by a "spirit of poorness"? Is it possible for materially rich persons to be characterized by a "spirit of poorness"? Do you know materially poor persons who are characterized by a "spirit of riches and power"?

3. In what sense should the disciples of Jesus feel "uncomfortable" in society? Is there some sense in which they should feel at home in the world?

4. What is the biblical meaning of "right-eousness"? What implications does this have for you and your congregation?

5. What does the apparent relationship between being merciful and obtaining mercy tell us about the nature and mission of the church?

6. What is necessary for a meek person to survive in our society? Do you agree with the statement that "the essential blessedness of the meek is too revolutionary to have been accepted by the Christian church"? If so, how would a Christian community characterized by "meekness" be different?

7. Integrity and sincerity are essential characteristics of the messianic community. Is this true of you? Of your congregation?

8. Do you agree that to be a peacemaker is to participate with God in His mission? What does it mean for you to be a peacemaker in your world?

9. Do you agree that in the first-century persecution simply confirmed the fact that the messianic community was living by kingdom values? How and where is this happening in our time?

10. How is the missionary visibility of the messianic community which is described in the Sermon on the Mount related to the witness and discipling mission which the various versions of the Great Commission mention? Can you cite any contemporary examples of this relationship?

11. Do you know of Christians or communities who try to be salt and light without living according to the values of the Sermon on the Mount? What are the results?

12. In what sense may law and gospel be antithetical categories? In what sense are they congenial and complementary? Why isn't the law-gospel antithesis very useful for understanding the Sermon on the Mount?

13. Do you think that it is appropriate to call Jesus radical? If so, in what sense?

14. Do you think that love is an adequate moral motivation for Christians? If not, what more is needed?

Chapter 5

# The Righteousness of the Kingdom (Matthew 5:21-48)

After Jesus lists the values that characterize the kingdom which He brought (Matthew 5:3-12), He points out that the quality of life which is lived in the messianic community reflects the very nature of God (Matthew 5:13-16). In reality, the values of the kingdom are expressions of the law of God carried to their fulfillment in His Messiah (Matthew 5:17-20).

Now, through a series of representative examples, Jesus shares His vision of the social relationships which characterize life in the kingdom. These examples by no means exhaust the possibilities. The list does not pretend to be inclusive, but contains a series of concrete pointers which describe the character of life within the messianic community.

Six times in this section of the Sermon on the Mount we find the phrase, "it was said . . . but I say to you." In this way Jesus presents radical new approaches to problems which resisted solution when they were tackled in traditional ways. These include the problem of anger (5:21-26), the problem of marital infidelity (5:27-30), the problem of divorce (5:31-32), the problem of falsehood (5:33-37), the problem of vengeance (5:38-42), and the problem of hatred toward one's enemies (5:43-48). In each case the formulation is negative in that the problem, as such, is taken as the point of discussion. Here, as well as in the Decalogue, we find solutions to attitudes and actions which have no place in the life of the people of God. However, in their impact, the teachings of Jesus are positive because they point toward a life characterized by peace, respect for one another and mutual confidence, trustworthiness, veracity, redemptive attitudes toward offenders, and love toward all, even those who are enemies.

### *The problem of anger (Matthew 5:21-26)*

The phrase "you have heard that it was said to men of old" is probably a reference to the traditional teachings which the first-century Jews received in an oral form in their synagogues. Verse 21 is a clear reference to the sixth commandment of the Decalogue (Exodus 20:13; Deuteronomy 5:17) in which homicide was absolutely forbidden. According to Hebrew custom a person accused of homicide was to be judged before the criminal court, or the "little sanhedrin," made up of twenty-three men. Of course this Old Testament provision reflects considerable progress over the type of anarchic situation in which personal vengeance was exacted.

"But I say to you," of verse 22, introduces the radicalization which Jesus gives to this commandment. It corresponds to a vision for its fulfillment which goes to the very root (radix) of God's intention for life together within the covenant community. The use of the term "brother" four times in three verses (22-24)) seems to indicate that Jesus is dealing with interpersonal relationships within the context of the messianic community. The disciples of Jesus will not merely abstain from committing homicide, they will refrain from all expressions of anger which are also ways of destroying their brother. Jesus understood very well that anger is the seed that can lead to homicide, when it matures. And anger in all of its forms leads to the destruction of integrity in interpersonal relationships. Wrath destroys brotherhood.

The three representative expressions of wrath mentioned in verse 22 are apparently meant to be understood in terms of increasing seriousness:

*"Every one who is angry with his brother shall be liable to judgment."* This implies that, in terms of seriousness, nursing anger toward another needs to be evaluated in the same way that homicide was judged under the traditional structures, by the criminal court. Jesus gives us to understand that a passion which may well ripen into homicide, by nursing it, is the root of murder and should be dealt with just as seriously as homicide. In this way Jesus reformulates the old law, placing it on a higher level which more fully corresponds to the intention of God. The verb translated here "is angry" is the same term employed in that seemingly strange text found in Ephesians 4:26, "Be angry, but do not sin." Here the verb can be indicative as well as imperative and is probably better translated as in *The New English Bible*, "If you are angry, do not let anger lead you into sin; do not let sunset find you still nursing it; leave no loop-hole for the devil."

*"Whoever insults his brother shall be liable to the council."* In this case "council" probably refers to the Sanhedrin, which in first-century Judaism was a supreme court. The term of abuse here translated "insults" is really the word *"raca"* and means something like "imbecile" or "crazy" or "stupid." In other words, it is a genuine insult to one's brother. Anger which is not only harbored but nurtured by insulting attitudes and words is even more dangerous and should be treated with even more seriousness, i.e., by taking it to a higher court.

*"Whoever says, 'you fool!' shall be liable to the hell of fire."* This is literally "the Gehenna of fire," a ravine on the edge of Jerusalem in which sacrifices to Molech were offered in earlier days. This became a symbol of judgment and perdition. The term translated "fool" was an extremely serious insult among the Jews. It amounted to calling one a "renegade" which in effect meant cutting him/her off from the people of God. This is the culmination of the process which begins with anger and is nurtured with insults. To be cut off from the Israel of God was to be condemned to death. And to be excluded from the messianic community means being bereft of any hope of salvation.

In all of their degrees of intensity, attitudes and expressions which do not contribute to the well-being of the brother or sister are forbidden in the community of the Messiah. Although the Christian church, as well as ancient Israel, consistently opposed homicide in its literal form, its defense of Jesus' radicalization of this principle has not been entirely free from ambiguity.

There is a widespread tendency to overlook many destructive forms which the expression of anger takes in social relationships. Popular psychology encourages people to "get their feelings out," to express anger for the sake of one's emotional health, often without regard for the destructive impact anger may have on others. Jesus' words forbid this lack of concern for brothers and sisters.

On the other hand, Christians may be tempted to deny anger. Jesus wants His disciples to be free from anger, not to deny it when it does appear. Other passages indicate that when anger and hurt feelings crop up, they should be dealt with immediately, before they victimize and become unmanageable.

The community of Jesus Christ has at its disposal resources which contribute to the spiritual and emotional health of its members in handling anger honestly and responsibly rather than with damaging outbursts and insults. The need for self-expression and emotional release is subordinate to concern for the salvation of brothers and sisters. In fact, according to verses 23 and 24, restored, healed relationships among brothers and sisters in the family of God are more important than external forms of worship. In order to keep anger and its bitter fruits from taking root in His community, Jesus gives two practical suggestions (4:23-25):

*First be reconciled to your brother.* As soon as persons become conscious that they have committed an offense, they should take the initiative to become reconciled with the offended one, even though it may mean interrupting an act of worship in its highest moment. True worship is possible only within a community of reconciled brothers and sisters (23, 24). For a Jew, worship is the highest and the holiest action a person can perform. But even worship is dependent upon restored relationships. By this Jesus affirms, beyond a shadow of doubt, the primacy of relationships which are fraternal over religious duties which are cultic. This, again, represents a more radical reformulation of the law.

*Make friends quickly with your accuser.* Personal offenses should be clarified, confessed, and forgiven concretely and without delay. In reality this is the meaning which the grammatical form of the verb (present participle), translated in verse 25 "make friends," conveys. Taking the initiative immediately in the direction of reconciliation may avoid the kind of situation which develops when offenses degenerate into attitudes of animosity and outright conflict emerges. This is also the way to protect the offended brother or sister against the temptation to become angry at the offender. The counsel offered by Paul, apparently in a similar situation, sheds light on the meaning of this text. "Do not let the sun go down on your anger, and give no opportunity to the devil" (Ephesians 4:26b, 27). In this counsel Paul reflects the Spirit of Jesus. The rapid resolution of animosities keeps them from flowering and producing their bitter harvest. In fact, allowing them to persist from one day to the next is, in effect, letting the devil have his way. And this, concretely, is the way in which anger becomes sin (Ephesians 4:26a).

### *The problem of marital infidelity (Matthew 5:27-30)*

In verse 27 Jesus refers to the seventh commandment, which forbids adultery (Exodus 20:14; Deuteronomy 5:18). It should not surprise us that two of the six representative problems which Matthew has included in this collection of Jesus' teachings deal with relationships between the sexes (adultery and divorce). This was a matter of great concern among the Jews of the first century. Furthermore, it represented one of the principal points of ethical conflict between Judaic Christianity and Greco-Roman culture. Paul's letters to the Corinthians provide abundant evidence of this conflict.

In His radicalization of this commandment Jesus used the tenth commandment to show that coveting the neighbor's wife, in effect, already makes one an adulterer (Exodus 20:17; Deuteronomy 5:21). By pointing out that adultery already exists in the act of coveting the neighbor's wife, Jesus defines the problem in fundamental Hebrew concepts. It is not merely a matter of personal sexual purity, as dualistic Greek categories of thought have taught us to formulate the problem, but rather an act which affects the well-being of another person—the neighbor. This was the typical Jewish way to weigh this kind of ethical action. It is not simply a possibility of losing one's own purity—which motivates the disciple of Jesus to avoid at all levels the temptation to marital infidelity; the motive is rather one's concern for the well-being of the other person. The Christian will avoid wronging both husband and wife, by avoiding the temptation to destroy their conjugal union.

It is clear that the teaching of Jesus, as well as the references from the Decalogue, are directed to men in their relationships with married women. Undoubtedly this way of stating the problem is due to the patriarchal social organization which predominated in ancient Israel, as well as in first-century Judaism. Under this system a woman's social life was determined by her relationship to a man, her father or her husband. Mark 10:12, on the other hand, recognizes the possibility that a woman may take the initiative in a divorce, a thing which would not be possible in Jewish society. This probably means that the Gospel of Mark reflects a non-Jewish situation in which civil law permitted a woman to divorce her husband. Certainly in the social organization which characterizes modern Western society, the words of Jesus would be directed to women as well as to men. In our day both women and men have legal recourse to divorce and thus either has the power to destroy the conjugal union of others, or harm through sexual cupidity. To the complex of relationships Jesus brings a clear word: harm not the other's union. Jesus recognizes the power of temptation and again goes to the root of the issue to offer the solution.

Verse 28 does not refer to a passing glance of admiration, but rather to a covetous and lustful look. As in the case of homicide, Jesus shows that the root of the offense lies in fundamental intention. Therefore to scrutinize a person with lascivious and covetous desire is *to be* an adulterer. Jesus talks about the act as committing adultery in one's heart. The heart in Hebrew thought obviously refers to more than the physical organ. What we notice less quickly is that it also does not refer narrowly to one's emotions. The Hebrew understanding of heart is much broader and deeper and more inclusive than physical and emotional life. The heart was seen as the seat of physical life and the emotions, but also of the intellect and will, the point of contact with God, virtually the equivalent of personality.° The kind of sin Jesus refers to here has its intentionality at the very center of human life.

But physical dimensions are not ignored. Jesus was concretely interested in the way in which the body's parts reflect the person's intentions. Verses 29 and 30 should not be summarily dismissed as a mere Semitic hyperbole. They remind us how important the members of our bodies are for us to function as persons. Even as sin is capable of exercising control over heart and mind, the body's members of necessity become sin's immediate instruments. Plucking out one's eye would not guarantee a victory over the inner springs of concupiscence. Instead, Jesus would have His disciples understand that the members of their bodies should respond to the sound impulses of the heart—in the best interests of the neighbor—rather than opening themselves to evil.

These verses leave no doubt concerning the priorities of Jesus. The authentic practice of the righteousness of the kingdom should occupy the full attention of the disciple. It is a very serious thing to offend or to harm one's neighbor! The profound concern of Jesus for the total person is made abundantly clear in these verses. It is not merely the lot of the soul, or of the heart, which interests Jesus here, but also the body. Jesus would have us to know that God is profoundly concerned about real people in their relationships with their neighbors.

*The problem of divorce (Matthew 5:31-32)*
Here Jesus refers to the Mosaic provision for the protection

---

° *Interpreter's Dictionary of the Bible*, Vol. 2, 549-50.

of a woman who had been repudiated by her husband (Deuteronomy 24:1). Here, as in the preceding paragraph, Jesus' purpose is to defend the integrity of marriage; there it was against marital infidelity, and here, against divorce, whatever the reason might be. In first-century Judaism there was a theological school which interpreted the Mosaic legislation in its most inclusive sense. Over against this school the teaching of Jesus defends the evangelical ideal, the ideal which is reflected in the Gospels, of the indissolubility of marriage. The line of thought which is developed in Matthew 19:3-12; Mark 10:1-12; and Luke 16:18 is implicit in this passage as well. Christians throughout the history of the church have debated the meaning of the conditional clause, "except on the ground of unchastity" (also in Matthew 19:9) asking if, in this exceptional case, Jesus does not indeed permit divorce and a new marriage in the messianic community.

In response it should be remembered that Jesus' teachings forbidding divorce are unconditional in the parallel passages in Mark 10:11, 12 and Luke 16:18. Indeed, if Jesus had intended to teach that marital infidelity is a legitimate grounds for divorce and remarriage in His community, He would have been no more radical in His understanding of God's intention for conjugal relationship in the family than the Jewish rabbi, Shammai, whose conservative school held that the only legitimate cause for divorce was adultery. One cannot help but notice, even in the Matthean passages which include an exception clause, that Jesus seems to be much more interested in safeguarding the indissolubility of marriage according to the primal intention of God expressed in creation itself (Matthew 19:6; Mark 10:6, 8, 9), than in granting some exception which would make divorce permissible. In fact, some propose the hypothesis that the exception clause reflects the situation of the church approximately one generation later when Matthew gathered this material together in the form in which it appears in his Gospel.

The term translated "unchastity" in verse 32 (and in Matthew 19:9) was also used by the Jewish rabbis to designate an illegitimate union, such as those forbidden in Leviticus 18. Therefore it might be this type of union which is referred to in the exception clause. With this meaning the phrase could be translated somewhat literally: "Everyone who dismisses his wife—except in the case of an illegitimate union—makes her commit adultery." This interpretation would seem to conform better to the Jewish background of Matthew's Gospel. This fact would also help us to understand the absence of the exception clause in Mark and Luke, since these Gospels appear to have been directed more specifically to non-Jewish readers.

Jesus, following the line of the authentic prophets (Malachi 2:14-16), insists on the sacred character of the marriage covenant because this reflects the true intention of God for the life of His people. We should not understand Jesus' teaching on divorce as a code intended for legislating public morality in a sovereign state. Legislation which merely imposes the formal indissolubility of marriage finds itself unable to promote marital fidelity and is therefore not a satisfactory solution to the problem. The Sermon on the Mount reflects an ethic of grace and is intended for disciples of Jesus in the context of the messianic community.

Of course these teachings of Jesus which deal with the marital relationships of men and women are also highly relevant for the life of the people of God in twentieth-century society. In the face of the rapid disintegration of marriage and the nuclear family which is a genuine threat in an already fragmented world, the teachings of Jesus stand as a clear defense of innocent children, as well as men and women who so easily fall prey to the selfish designs of others. In a society oriented toward the perverted exploitation of sex for selfish purposes, we do well to remember the fundamental concern which Jesus expressed for the well-being of the neighbor. We should remember that all of these basically selfish perversions of sex carry within themselves the seeds of destruction. Pornography, for example, which encourages sexual gratification in the unreal and imaginary world of fantasy proves in the end to be frustrating and destructive. Those sexual practices which are oriented exclusively in the satisfaction of the self-centered impulses of the individual deny, in reality, the basically social functions of sex. In the end those, too, prove to be illusory. The promiscuity with which relationships are entangled in liberal Western societies turns into a mockery and the true realization of personhood so desperately sought continues to elude its practitioners.

All of these and other basically selfish perversions of sex run contrary to the best counsels of our history: against the witness of ancient Israel (Deuteronomy 22:22), against the practice and teachings of Jesus (Matthew 15:19), against the teachings of the early church (1 Corinthians 6:9, 10; Galatians 5:19; Ephesians 5:3, 5), and against the experience of human societies in general, because they do not contribute to true personal well-being nor to authentically satisfying social relationships.

We live in a culture which overrates the experience of intercourse and exaggerates its importance for self-expression, fulfillment, and meeting physical need. Increasingly, people in our society find it hard to conceive of celibacy as a serious option for healthy people. In the context of this kind of society, Jesus' followers face a real challenge to demonstrate that affectionate, familial relationships within the messianic community contribute far more to personal and corporate well-being than promiscuous encounters. In such a community the contributions, needs, and potential for wholeness of all people, married and single, can be recognized. The exaggerated attention to erotic aspects of love and sex is replaced by appreciation of the place of celibacy as well as appreciation for the proper place of intercourse within permanent lifelong covenant.

Modern Western Christians generally seek their social and spiritual security in the biological family, more than in the family of God. But in reality, the nuclear family has become little more than the extension of individual selfishness. In this context the community of the Messiah bears witness that God has acted in human history to create a new social entity, the family of God, which gathers up and transcends the possibilities for human well-being found in the biological family. It is here that true salvation is experienced. It is here that self-centered individualism, clannish tribalism, and proud nationalism are overcome. It is here that we find true life in laying down our lives for one another (Matthew 10:37-39).

### The problem of falsehood (Matthew 5:33-37)

Another of the instructions, which Jesus said the forefathers had received from their teachers, was a law forbidding the swearing of false oaths. Instead they were to keep all of the promises they made under oath in which they invoked God as a witness. It is difficult to know exactly which part of the Old Testament served as a basis for this rabbinic instruction. Numbers 30:3, 4; Deuteronomy 23:21, and Ecclesiasties 5:2-4 are probably examples of the practice to which reference is made.

In this case Jesus radicalizes the prohibition of perjury by pointing out that it is the intention of God that persons should always be truthful in their communication with others. In fact this eliminates the need for swearing oaths. In the new ethic which Jesus teaches, truthfulness is assured, not through the external means of an oath, but through the inner integrity of the person. The oath, by its very nature, implies the dishonest character of the person who swears and an essential lack of trust in the one who accepts the oath. Therefore in the messianic community where evil in general, and dishonesty in particular, are not taken for granted, the oath is out of place.

According to Jesus, all oaths are wrong in the messianic community in which interpersonal relationships are characterized by sincerity; where "yes" means yes and "no" means no (James 5:12). In fact, in the community of Christ all superfluous words are out of place. In the body of Christ words take on their full meaning and language is used with sobriety. Communication is employed with modesty in the interests of the common good (James 3:1-12). It is only within the community of the Messiah that unchecked communication can be stripped of the demonic dimensions of the power which it has usurped and unmasked as the giant evil that it has become in our world. In this community, communication is characterized by the simple and unostentatious way in which truth is spoken. In fact, Jesus warns that "anything more than this comes from [the] evil [one]" (37). This is probably a reference to Satan, "the father of lies," but it also warns us of the demonic power of propaganda in our world. Due to the fundamentally mendacious nature of interpersonal relationships in society, the oath has become a "necessity" in public life. But in the messianic community simple, sincere, truthful communication has rendered the oath obsolete.

Falsehood and deceit, on one hand, and transparent sincerity, on the other, characterize two kingdoms which are fundamentally opposed. Even though veracity is an extremely rare virtue in society, in His community Jesus expects His disciples to be sincere. However, this does not mean that we are free to be brutal in our candor, nor dare we exercise cruelty in our concern for truth. Among the followers of Jesus the truth is spoken in love (Ephesians 4:15).

*The problem of vengeance (Matthew 5:38-42)*
In the fifth example which He evokes, Jesus reminds His followers that another of the Old Testament teachings which the rabbis have been repeating in the synagogues is the so-called "law of talion" (in Latin, *talis* means "such as" or "like" or "so"; in other words, the retaliation is limited to being *like* the offense) (Leviticus 24:20). The form which this provision took in popular instruction was simply "an eye for an eye and a tooth for a tooth" (Exodus 21:24; Leviticus 24:20; Deuteronomy 19:20). Although in these Old Testament passages the rigor of the punishment is sometimes underscored, we should remember that this provision constituted a notable improvement over the anarchic system in which unrestricted personal vengeance was taken. An example of this attitude can be found in Lamech, whose practically unlimited desire for vengeance bore little relation to the original offense (Genesis 4:23, 24). In reality the talion principle was a measure designed to protect the offender against disproportionate retaliation. It was an ancient attempt to keep the spiral of violence under control. Of course, this provision was not limited to ancient Israel.

Similar measures appear in Ancient Near Eastern legislation, such as the code of Hammurabi, about 1,800 years before the time of Jesus.

In His radicalization of this principle Jesus says to His disciples, "Do not resist one who is evil" (39). With this statement Jesus moves beyond all other positions before Him, which were known to have been taken toward evildoers. A possible exception might be found in some of the concepts found in the Suffering Servant Songs of Isaiah. Although exhortations to exercise patience toward others and to practice mutual aid were well known in Judaism, Jesus' global condemnation of the spirit of litigation and retaliation and His willingness to suffer unjustly rather than to inflict suffering, such as we find in this text, were totally unknown. In effect, Jesus has introduced into human society a new norm for determining social relationships. This ethic of the kingdom, which Jesus declares is already in effect among His disciples, shows up the utter insufficiency inherent in the law of talion with which the established authorities attempt to order human relationships within organized societies. It is simply incapable of providing the basis upon which humankind can live together in real peace.

It has been alleged that the ethic which we find in the Sermon on the Mount is strictly individual. And it is further claimed that in order to elaborate a social ethic capable of restraining evil human impulses, it is necessary to fall back on the law of talion. But in reality, it is not a matter of a personal ethic (the Sermon on the Mount) in opposition to a social or collective ethic (the law of talion). Here the new morality of the kingdom which is individual as well as collective is placed over against the ethic of the established social order which, in reality, participates in "this present evil age" and is therefore destined to pass away.

To "not resist one who is evil" in reality means that a person will love and do good to the evildoer, even though one steadfastly opposes evil. This idea of not resisting one who is evil, of not responding to evil persons with violence or a spirit of retaliation, was so novel and so revolutionary that Jesus found it necessary to employ four examples to illustrate the principle. The identity of "the evil one" is further clarified in the examples which follow: "anyone [who] strikes you" (39b); "anyone [who] would sue you" (40); "anyone [who] forces you" (41); and anyone "[who] begs from you" (42).

These four concrete examples which follow should not be understood as rules in a legal sense, but rather as samples of the way in which the principle which Jesus spoke can be applied. In fact they were practical examples of the kind of situations which Jesus' hearers were likely to experience but they certainly do not exhaust the meaning or the consequences of the principle "Do not resist one who is evil."

Although this fact generally escapes readers of English versions of the New Testament, it should also be noted that whereas the principle is given in the second person plural (39a), the four examples which follow (39b, 40, 41, 42) are all formulated in the second person singular (you, your). It would seem that Jesus (and the teachers in the church who used the Sermon on the Mount in the Christian communities for whom Matthew prepared his Gospel) wants each disciple to discover personally the consequences of the application of this principle to his life. This reminds us of the concern, so characteristic of the Jews, for translating the will of God into the concrete aspects of the daily life of people.

*If anyone strikes you.* The first of these examples is drawn from the field of interpersonal relationships. "But if any one strikes you on the right cheek, turn to him the other also" (39b). To strike a person on the cheek with the back of one's hand (in this case a right-handed person would necessarily tap the other person on his *right* cheek) constituted a most offensive form of insulting another person in the ancient world. In fact, this is still the case in the Near East. In the blow here described, the problem is not so much a matter of physical harm, but rather the humiliating insult which one has received. Jesus teaches that His disciples should accept one insult after another without returning the affront. This comportment corresponds exactly with the prophetic vision of the Suffering Servant of Yahweh (Isaiah 50:6) and to the attitude which Jesus Himself later showed (Matthew 26:67; Mark 14:65).

*If anyone would sue you.* The second example is drawn from the field of legal relationships. "If any one would sue you and take your coat, let him have your cloak as well" (40). Here Jesus is saying that His disciples will not respond violently to those persons who demand something which does not belong to them. In fact, they will treat their adversary with generosity. We should not think of this as an idealistic ethic which was therefore never attempted in the primitive community. Although it was true, as the rabbinic tradition points out, that a craze for litigation existed in Palestine in Jesus' time and even increased in later years, the attitude of the apostles on this matter was clear. In the instructions which he sent to the church in Corinth, Paul shows that he had understood perfectly well the Spirit of Jesus (1 Corinthians 6:7, 8). Living in the midst of Hellenistic society in which litigation was a common practice, Paul warns that it is preferable to suffer wrong, and even to be defrauded, than to sue one's neighbor, even with just cause. In the example which Jesus used there is no question that justice would have been on the side of the disciple, since the law protected the poor and forbade despoiling him of his garment (Exodus 22:25 f.; Deuteronomy 24:12 f.).

*If anyone forces you.* The third example is taken from the realm of political relationships. "If any one forces you to go one mile, go with him two miles" (41). In this case Jesus is referring to the right of government officials to exact forced labor from their subjects. In the time of Jesus, Palestine was a colony within the Roman Empire. Imperial officials and soldiers in the forces of occupation could require any passerby that came along to carry their baggage, or to accompany them as a hostage or a guide. It is not difficult to imagine what the attitude of the Jews in general toward these representatives of an oppressive foreign regime must have been. Precisely for this reason, this example is all the more noteworthy, indeed, daring.

Jesus says that His disciples will render the services which are required; in fact, they will even go beyond that which is imposed. In no sense do they do this in order to express their approval of the injustices which were committed by the oppressors. Neither were they collaborating in the oppression. It was rather a concrete expression of concern for the well-being of that particular person who required their help, even though he be a hated member of the foreign legion or an imperial official—persons who were generally considered enemies of the Jewish people. It was a concrete way of responding to the violence of oppression with genuine goodness and loving concern for the other person. It was a way of breaking the spiral of violence.

*Give to him who begs.* The fourth example is taken from the field of economic relationships. "Give to him who begs from you, and do not refuse him who would borrow from you" (42). The context would lead us to imagine that this "begging" and "borrowing" has to do with a somewhat violent demand which is not based on the legitimate claim of the person who insists. This is the idea which one gets from the Lukan parallel: "Give to everyone who asks you, and do not ask for your property back from the man who robs you" (6:30, *The Jerusalem Bible*). In this context verse 42 does not call so much for an act of mutual aid or of brotherly love, as it does a gesture of pacification and an attitude of patience in response to the violence of another. The virtues which characterize the disciple of Jesus here are generosity, good will, and patience.

Jesus clearly forbids His disciples to avenge themselves. Then He offers them four examples of what the application of a spirit free from vengeance might mean in their daily lives. Certainly there will be other situations in which they will be able to show that they have been liberated from a vindictive attitude through the power of the Spirit of their Lord. This spirit, which characterized the personal activity of Jesus, as well as of His disciples, was radically new and revolutionary. But it is an attitude which has the power to transform interpersonal relationships. Paul caught perfectly well this intention of Jesus, as we can see from what he wrote to the Christians in Rome, "Do not be overcome by evil, but overcome evil with good" (Romans 12:21). And, above all, we should remember that this is the way in which God has responded to a rebellious world in the person of His Messiah. This is the strategy which God adopted to break the spiral of violence in its most vicious form.

### The problem of hatred of enemies (Matthew 5:43-48)

In the sixth of these representative instructions Jesus reminds His disciples that they have been taught to love their neighbors and to hate their enemies (43). The command to love one's neighbor was well known in the Old Testament (Leviticus 19:18) and it formed a part of Jesus' summary of "all the law and the prophets" (Matthew 22:37-40). However, the second part of this traditional teaching, "hate your enemy," does not occur anywhere in the Old Testament, at least not explicitly.

It has been suggested that this phrase came to be included in religious instruction among the Jews because of the idea that all those who did not belong to the national and religious community of the Jews were, in fact, enemies of God and His people. It was this fact that justified the "holy hatred" of God's people. In fact, this hatred does not seem so much to be personal and passionate, as it does collective and religious. In the context here in Matthew, it appears to be a natural response to persecution (Matthew 5:44; 10:22; 24:9).

But an even clearer explanation can probably be found in the attitude which the Essene community took toward their enemies. In many ways they were like Jesus in their approach to the law. They were serious about their insistence on obedience to its demands. They were also radically serious in their application of the Old Testament Scriptures. But their understanding of the nature of God led them to form a closed community which demanded hatred of those outside. This is the point at which Jesus and His community differed most fundamentally from the Essenes of His day. It has been suggested that this reference to hatred of enemies may well have been a direct allusion to the Essenes.

Jesus radicalizes the law which calls on persons to love their neighbors by extending it to include enemies. And furthermore, this love which Jesus commands is not merely the absence of hatred, or the spirit of vengeance. In tune with biblical thought in general, Jesus expects this love to be shown in action. Jesus charges His disciples to pray for their persecutors (44) and to greet their enemies, as well as their friends (47). But above all, the heavenly Father who "makes his sun rise on the evil and the good, and sends rain on the just and on the unjust" (45) best illustrates the kind of love which Jesus expects His followers to show.

In order to be in fact what they are in principle—children of God—Jesus calls on His disciples to love in the same way in which God loves—to be like their Father who is in heaven. While it is true that even pagans are capable of certain expressions of love which are motivated by their own self-interest, children of God are to love just as God loves, unselfishly and even self-sacrificially without questioning the worthiness of those who are the objects of His love (see Luke 6:34, 35).

*You, therefore, must be perfect, as your heavenly Father is perfect* (48). This statement is both a promise and a command. The disciples of the Messiah are to imitate their Father (as well as the Son) in the indiscriminating way in which they love. The children of God should resemble their Father in His way of loving. This text does not teach a doctrine of Christian perfectionism in some abstract or philosophical sense. Jesus is simply pointing out that the love of the disciple will be complete, or mature, or perfect, when it resembles the lavish and indiscriminate love of God. In the parallel passage in Luke, Jesus calls on His disciples to "be merciful, even as your Father is merciful" (6:36). The term "perfect," as it is used in this text, probably reflects the Hebrew concept of "wholeness" or "integrity." God has always expected integrity on the part of His people (Deuteronomy 18:13)—not, as often interpreted, a human striving for faultlessness. Love for one's enemies is an essential component of Christian comportment which insures its integrity. In fact, this is the fundamental difference which distinguishes it from all other "ethics."

*Love overcomes enmity.* In almost every sphere of human

relationships one observes the prominent role of "enmity" as a principle of social organization. Political alignments in the field of international relations seem to be oriented around the principles of ideological, sociopolitical, and economic competition. In more limited circles of interpersonal relationships, an enormous amount of energy is dedicated to competing with others. It almost seems as if we need someone against whom we can struggle. This tendency toward hostility is found in family relationships, in the ways in which we live together in the neighborhood, in the relations between labor and capital, and, we might as well admit it, in interpersonal relationships in Christian congregations. The struggles which divide us in the church are not generally based on real concerns about maintaining sound doctrine, nor are they the results of genuine ethical considerations. They are, rather, hostilities which are the products of personal self-interest.

Life in the messianic community will be different. To the degree in which the disciples of Jesus put into practice the principles of kingdom living, they can expect persecution—but they will not hate their persecutors. On the contrary, they will find concrete ways to show their love toward their enemies and to seek their well-being. The disciple of Jesus does not practice the way of love for pragmatic reasons, but simply because this is the way in which God acts.

This spirit of love, which refuses to resist evil persons on their own violent terms, finally dawned on Jesus' disciples—although apparently they did not catch the full vision until after Pentecost—and was practiced in the apostolic communities. This fact is clearly documented in the New Testament. But the Gospels show us how difficult it was for them to really grasp this revolutionary new vision of love. In fact they could not understand why Jesus did not organize and lead a violent uprising aimed at freeing God's people, Israel, from the foreign oppressor. However, they eventually came to realize that the clearest and fullest manifestation of God's redemptive love is found in the cross. The cross of Jesus was, in reality, the consequence of His nonresistant love for His enemies.

Throughout its history, and especially since the time of Constantine, the Christian church has given very little attention to the fundamental role of this radical love which should characterize the disciple of Jesus. The church has expended tremendous amounts of energy in the elaboration of confessions of faith in an effort to define that which is considered essential to belief. But about the way in which we are specifically expected to imitate God himself, in indiscriminating, unselfish, and sacrificial love, the church in general has had very little to say. Small minorities of believers within various groups throughout history, however, have resisted the pressures of society and loved as God loves. Their example gives us fresh courage in our day.

In the community of the Messiah, hatred toward the enemy is forbidden. Instead, following Jesus means accepting a cross. In the Gospels we read that Jesus took up His cross only after Pilate had passed sentence against Him. The cross is the symbol of the verdict of Jesus' enemies. And in the case of Jesus' disciples, their cross is also symbolic of the verdict which their enemies issue against them. To take up one's cross implies the willingness to absorb in oneself the violence of one's enemies, rather than taking vengeance on them. It is a way of loving and forgiving one's enemies, rather than hating and destroying them. In reality, the cross is the style of life which characterizes the disciple of Jesus.

## The kingdom come

In His radicalization of the "law and the prophets," Jesus offers a series of pointers which reveals the fundamental character of the kingdom community in which life responds to the intention of God for His people. Anger, unfaithfulness, falsehood, vengeance, and hatred in human relationships are all overcome in that community which is characterized by peace, respect for one another, mutual confidence, trustworthiness, sincerity, redemptive attitudes toward offenders, and unselfish love toward all, even those who are enemies.

These are the fundamental features of the community of the kingdom which has been inaugurated by the Messiah anticipating the reign of God over the entire universe, that will appear one day in all of its splendor.

*Questions for Discussion*

1. What does Jesus' radicalization of the sixth commandment do to the argument that since apparently only murder is forbidden there, other forms of violence are permitted under certain circumstances?

2. What are some of the implications of being Jesus' community in the midst of a society characterized by self-centered sexism?

3. What are the implications of the kingdom value of veracity in a world in which deception is considered "necessary" to survival?

4. Is Jesus' variety of nonresistance an antiquated and negative approach to conflict, or is it a daring new way to break through the vicious spiral of violence? Do you know people with the courage to respond to violent persons in this way? What are the implications of this principle in your relationships?

5. Do you think it is presumptuous to try to imitate God? What are the implications of Matthew 5:44, 45, 48 for the answer to this question?

6. Make a list of characteristics which you consider essential to relationships in the community which corresponds to God's intention for His people. Does this list describe any congregation or community you know personally?

# The Spirituality of the Kingdom (Matthew 6:1-34)

In the Sermon on the Mount Jesus has already described the character of kingdom citizens (5:3-12), the missionary visibility of the messianic community (5:13-16), the intimate relationship between Jesus' teachings and the intention of God for His people as it had been expressed in His law (5:17-20), and the righteousness of the kingdom crowned by a daring new ethic of love (5:21-48). The generous sprinkling of verbs in the imperative mood in this last section (21-48) invites the disciple of Jesus to decisive action along lines determined by the ethic of the kingdom.

In chapter 6 Jesus' teachings are directed toward the spiritual life of the community, which expresses its relationship to God. One is tempted to describe the contents of this chapter in terms of "vertical" relationships in contrast to "horizontal" ones. However, in Jesus' teaching, spiritual relationships have social dimensions and social matters are of spiritual consequence. The biblical understanding of spirituality is global and resists all human attempts to set up religious categories.

Jesus sets His instructions in the context of the religious practices current among the Jews of His time: almsgiving, prayer, and fasting. But Jesus also notes that a person's attitude toward property, in the context of God's exclusive right to the loyalty of

His people, plays a fundamental role in determining one's spirituality. Jesus confronts the religious practices of His contemporaries, characterized in terms of "hypocrisy" in the practice of almsgiving, prayer, and fasting (6:2, 5), and "anxiety" which showed itself in their attitude toward property and God's providence (6:7, 32-34).

### The practice of piety (6:1-18)

Verse 1 serves as an introduction to all of Jesus' teachings concerning the three common religious practices of His contemporaries: almsgiving (2-4), prayer (5-15), and fasting (16-18). In each of these cases we observe three common elements: there is a brief description of the ostentatious way in which piety is practiced by these "hypocrites"; there is an ironic affirmation of the reward which they receive from their peers; Jesus offers a description of the forms which the practice of authentic piety takes.

In this relation it is important to note that Jesus does not attack the practice of giving alms, of praying, and of fasting, as such. It is rather their perversion at the hands of these "hypocrites" which is submitted to such scathing criticism. Jesus apparently assumes that His disciples will continue these practices, because they are valid expressions of their relationship to God. But at the same time they are alerted to subtle dangers which are inherent in all practice of piety—hypocrisy.

At first sight, it might seem that these instructions contradict the descriptions of the missionary visibility of the messianic community which Jesus gave earlier (5:14-16). But this inconsistency is only superficial. The practice of one's piety should not be done out of a vain desire for ostentation. It should, on the other hand, be exemplary. If these practices correspond to motives which are sincere, they will be seen in the same sense that "a city on a hill cannot be hid" and will bring glory to God.

"*Beware of practicing your piety before men in order to be seen by them*" (1). The term, here translated "beware," is generally used in a polemic or negative sense in Matthew (7:15; 10:17; 16:6, 11, 12). Here it constitutes a serious warning against a

course of action which is entirely incompatible with the style of
life which characterizes the kingdom. The term here translated
"piety" is, in reality, the Greek word which is usually translated as
"righteousness" or "justice." In this case it refers to the entire con-
figuration of concrete actions and gestures, together with the corresponding attitudes, which express the reality of kingdom life.
Here, almsgiving, prayer, and fasting are three expressions of this
"righteousness" or "justice."

The constant temptation of humanity is to forget that we live
in relation to God and that, therefore, all of life must constantly be
submitted to the judgment of God (Matthew 10:32, 33; 25:32; 2
Corinthians 5:10). When this fact is forgotten, a person is liable to
attribute excessive importance to the judgment of other people.
When this happens one's religious practices become mere
"theater productions" put on in the presence of others. The Greek
verb here translated "to be seen" contains the root out of which
the English word "theater" has evolved. Jesus says, in effect, that
to seek the applause of our fellows in our religious practices will finally deprive us of the only approval that really matters: God's.
God does not share with mankind His prerogative to exercise
judgment. God has charged His community with the tasks of discernment and forgiveness of sins, but not judgment.

*Almsgiving (Matthew 6:2-4).* In verse 1 Jesus gives the principle which governs the practice of piety in His community.
Notice that the personal pronouns (you and your) occur in the
plural form (although this fact is not readily evident to English
readers). However, when Jesus deals with the specific practices of
alms (2-4), prayer (5, 6), and fasting (17, 18), He employs the singular form of the pronouns (you and your), with the exception of
verse 16. It seems that Jesus is interested in applying the teaching
to each of His disciples in particular so that its implementation
will be personal and concrete. We have already observed this
concern in our study of Matthew 5:39-42.

The giving of alms (the Greek term literally means "mercy")
was a sacred duty in ancient Israel. *"You shall open wide your*

*hand to your brother, to the needy and to the poor, in the land"*
(Deuteronomy 15:11c). And in Jesus' time Jewish legal provisions
on behalf of the poor were extensive in coverage and efficient in
practice. A powerful organization was busy everywhere collecting
alms in behalf of the disinherited and needy.

"Sound no trumpet" (2) is probably a figure of speech to
highlight the ridiculous lengths to which human religious vanity is
capable of going—although there is an ancient Jewish document
which reports the custom of announcing the hour of the collection
with a trumpet blast. It is possible to distinguish two different
kinds of "hypocrites" in Matthew's Gospel. There are, first of all,
hypocrites in the ordinary sense of the term. These are persons
who pretend to be pious, when in truth they are not. They maliciously pretend to be what they are not (see Matthew 15:7, 8;
22:18). The term is also used in a deeper and more pathetic sense
in which "hypocrites" are those who have deceived themselves in
their own game of religious vanity. These might be called
"sincère" hypocrites. These are the persons to whom Jesus refers
in this chapter and possibly also in Matthew 23:15, *et al.* According to Jesus, it would appear that a hypocrite is not just the person
who is conscious of being one. Jesus' listeners could not fail to
catch the irony of the final phrase in verses 2, 5, and 16, "they
have their reward." They have already received what they were
expecting—the admiration of other people—and this will lead
them to their ruin. They are the tragic victims of their own mis-
directed sincerity.

In verses 2, 5, and 16, the Greek verb in the phrase which is
translated "they have their reward" is really a commercial term
and indicates the receipt of payment in full. It appears in ancient
papyrus documents as a technical mercantile term. And as such it
appears on tax receipts of the period, "paid in full." However, it
should be noted that this verb is reserved for those texts which
refer to the reward given by men to those who, in their religious
practices, seek their approval. Although our translation does not
indicate it, a different verb is used to describe the reward which is
promised and given by God to those whose piety is authentic (4, 6,

18). God Himself is the One who offers this recompense and there is a correspondence between the religious and moral practices of disciples and the reward which God will heap upon them.

The counsel "do not let your left hand know what your right hand is doing" (3) does not mean that alms are to be given in a blind or irrational way. Jesus here calls for a total lack of concern for oneself in almsgiving. Alms are to be given for the well-being of the poor, and not for the inner satisfaction of the giver, and certainly not to make an impression on others. The poor and needy are the center of Jesus' concern and this should be no less true of His disciples.

The expression "so that your alms may be in secret" (4) could be understood in more than one sense: that no one else should know about it; or instead of giving your alms with spectators in mind, give your alms, keeping in mind only God who sees you and asks it of you, and the person who needs it. The second of these meanings probably offers the best interpretation. It is not so much a maneuver by which a magnanimous giver remains anonymous, as it is sincere concern, before God, for the brother or sister in need. Verses 17 and 18 would seem to confirm this interpretation. Fasting is a concrete and public act, in the sense that it is done in the midst of people. However, it is not done with observers in mind, but only with reference to God. Likewise, God will reward this concrete and public act in response to the practice of authentic piety on the part of the disciple.

*Prayer (Matthew 6:5-15).* Among the Jews of Jesus' time the practice of prayer was divided into three principal categories: prayer in the temple, prayer in the synagogues or other public places, and domestic or private prayer. In verses 5 and 6 Jesus apparently deals with the second of these categories. There were two principal characteristics which particularly distinguished Jewish prayer. The first was a clear consciousness of dependence on the sovereign mercy of God. And the second was a clear concept of the close relationship which exists between the practice of prayer and life as it is concretely lived. This meant that for a pious Jew there was hardly an hour of his conscious existence in which he did not offer prayer to God. As might be expected, this fundamental role of prayer in the daily life of the Jews became the occasion for endless discussion about conditions under which it was appropriate to pray and endless attempts to regulate the practice of prayer. This was the complex situation which so easily lent itself to abuse in Jesus' time.

The prayers of the "hypocrites" (5), against which Jesus warned His disciples, were not simulated prayers. These prayers were apparently sincere, but they were offered by a person praying at the same time for show in public. In other words, the pray-er was a "sincere" hypocrite. The "room" to which Jesus refers in verse 6 was probably the chamber of an ordinary Palestinian house. These were sometimes used to store grain or other provisions and more often than not the house of a poor family would have only one room. In verse 6 Jesus does not recommend silence or solitude, for their own sakes, as proper conditions for prayer. He insists, rather, on the absence of admirers of one's practice of prayer. We should not imagine that God can be more easily approached in solitude than He can in the street, or in the synagogue, or in the temple. Jesus teaches that it is necessary to seek the presence of God rather than the presence and admiration of one's fellows. And the presence of God is to be found, above all, in the context of community (Matthew 18:19, 20; Acts 4:24; *et al.*) Jesus does not recommend solitude for its own sake, but for the sake of avoiding the human tendency to put oneself on display—show off.

*The attitude toward prayer (Matthew 6:7, 8).* Up to this point in His teachings concerning the spirituality of the kingdom (6:1-6, 16-18), Jesus has shown the contrast which exists between the practice of piety in the messianic community and the religious practices of the scribes and Pharisees, which are characterized by hypocrisy (6:2, 5, 16). In relation to their practice of prayer and their attitudes toward property, the orientation of the disciples of Jesus is contrasted with the attitude of "the Gentiles" (6:7, 32). The problem of these pagans, in their approach to prayer as well as in their attitude toward property, consists of anxiety about the provision of their material needs. Just as hypocrisy is the prime temptation of religious people, now Jesus adds that anxiety, or worry about material provisions, is essentially a pagan temptation. Perhaps this is a criterion by which we can determine if we are really people of God, or if we entertain the anxiety of pagans.

The anxiety of the pagans leads them to offer long prayers filled with words which, in reality, are empty and meaningless. Of course the length of the prayer, as such, is not really the problem. The difficulty lies in the fact that they imagine that their repetition and wordiness will somehow exert pressure on God, causing Him to respond favorably.

The remedy for this pagan anxiety is to simply recognize that God is a "Father who knows" (6:8, 32) and is concerned about the needs of His children. Nevertheless, Jesus teaches His followers to ask for what they need with simplicity and humble confidence (6:11, 25-34). Jesus teaches that prayer in His community will be sober, modest, and spontaneous.

While it is true that in contrast to the practice of his contemporaries, the Jews and the Essenes, Jesus is not reported in the Gospels assigning special times, or hours, for prayer, this, of course, does not necessarily mean that Jesus and His followers discontinued Jewish disciplines of prayer. Quite to the contrary, Luke reports members of the primitive community "going up to the temple at the hour of prayer" (Acts 3:1) and the Acts of the Apostles and the epistles describe a community in which the discipline of prayer is a joyful privilege (Acts 1:14; 2:42; 6:4; 16:16; James 5:16; Revelation 5:8; et al.)

However, sobriety in the practice of prayer does not necessarily imply mediocrity or poverty of expression. The absence of daily stipulated times for prayer does not imply an absence of spiritual discipline. Prayer in the community of Jesus is the free and spontaneous expression of children who have learned to trust their Father fully.

If God already knows all of our needs, why pray? In reality, if prayer consisted merely of informing God of our needs there would probably be no need for prayer. But Jesus teaches that our relationship to God is that of children to their Father. And in this highly personal relationship, communication plays a fundamentally important role. God wants to relate to us as persons, as sons and daughters. Therefore, praise, adoration, thanksgiving, confession, intercession, petition, and every other expression of our love for God are of fundamental importance. It is in this context that the teaching of Jesus known as "the Lord's Prayer" serves as a model for our practice of prayer.

*The Lord's Prayer* (6:9-13). The Lord's Prayer is probably a list of suggestions offered by Jesus for the instruction of His disciples, rather than a liturgical formula to be recited. As we see in the epistles of Paul and the Acts of the Apostles, the Lord's Prayer was surely not understood as the only legitimate form for prayer among Jesus' followers. While the spirit of the Lord's Prayer was taken over by the New Testament community, the form of prayer in the gathered community was free and functional. Prayer was a living drama (Acts 4:23-31).

There are six petitions in the Lord's Prayer (or seven, if we divide verse 13 into two separate requests). The first three have to do with God and are therefore essentially praise or adoration. The last three refer to the elemental needs of humankind, and are therefore supplication or petition. In the Lord's Prayer there is a concentration on that which is really essential to life in the messianic community. Therefore reflection on these teachings will be instructive, not only for our understanding of prayer, but for our comprehension of life in the community of the Messiah.

To be able to address God as "Father" constitutes the first and greatest element of prayer. Although it was common in Jewish prayers of the time to call on God as Father, the practice in the primitive Christian community surely owes its origin to Jesus. In the synoptic Gospels, Jesus refers to God as His Father in a way which is highly significant (see, for example Matthew 5:16, 48; 6:1, 4, 8, 14, 15; 7:11; 10:20, 29; 13:34; 18:14; 23:9.) The dominant motifs which one observes in these passages are: God is a Father who cares for His children with tender loving care; He is the one who will judge them on the last day. In other words, the Judge before whom we will stand on the final day is the same Father whom we already know through Jesus. God is the Father of Jesus, the Messiah (Matthew 11:25; 15:13; 16:17), and He is at the same time, by virtue of the eschatological kingdom which has been inaugurated by Jesus, Father of all those who participate in this messianic kingdom. Therefore, the possessive "*our* Father" in the prayer undoubtedly refers to the messianic community, to the disciples of Jesus and to all those "disciples" who will eventually participate in the blessedness of the kingdom. The context in which it is set warns us against reading universalistic nuances into the term, "*our* Father."

In the primitive messianic community the invocation of God as Father took on a degree of intimacy completely unknown among the Jews of this period. They were accustomed to substituting the term "heaven" for "God" in order to avoid pronouncing the divine name. In contrast, the apostolic church was accustomed to using the familiar Aramaic expression of intimate affection, "Abba" (Galatians 4:6; Romans 8:15; 14:36). However, among the Jews this term was never applied to God. It was limited, instead, to the most intimate family relationships, such as that which little children might enjoy with their fathers. Therefore, the modern equivalent of "abba" would probably be "daddy," or a similar term of endearment. It was surely from Jesus Himself that the disciples learned to use this term of familiar affection and to apply it to their Father, a really daring thing to do in the socio-religious environment of first-century Judaism. (See Matthew 11:26; John 5:36; 11:25, 27; 26:29, 42, 53.)

"*Hallowed be thy name*" (9b). In effect, the messianic community is asking that the nature and intention of God be revealed and realized in the midst of humankind. God hallows His name in human history through the community which worships Him. In reality, this first petition anticipates and incorporates all those which follow: the coming of the kingdom, the fulfillment of God's will, the life of the messianic community on earth with its need of bread, forgiveness, and liberation. All of these concerns are present in essence, in the petition that the "name" of God (that is, His character, His nature, His will) be revealed, recognized, reverenced, and obeyed among all people.

*Thy kingdom come* (10a). Another way of expressing this petition would be: "Bring in the kingdom which you have promised to us." In his Gospel, Matthew uses the verb which is translated here "come" to designate both the historic coming of the Messiah in the person of Jesus of Nazareth (3:11; 5:17; 9:13), as well as Jesus' final appearing in the awaited Parousia (16:27, 28; 24:30, 42; 25:10). According to Matthew's Gospel in the historic coming of Jesus the kingdom of God has drawn near in a definitive sense (3:2; 10:7). This kingdom has been announced and persons are invited to enter it, because, in effect, Jesus has inaugurated it in His person. And thanks to the clear signs which Jesus has given to His followers, it is possible to know the nature of this kingdom and to look forward in confidence to its fulfillment.

When Jesus' followers pray that the "kingdom come," they are not asking for some completely unknown and new thing. The kingdom of God is at hand in the person of Jesus and participation in this kingdom requires radical repentance (Matthew 4:17). The Sermon on the Mount furnishes a summary of the values which characterize life in this kingdom. But although Jesus has inaugurated this kingdom, it still awaits its full and definitive establishment at the end of human history. This is the vision which leads the disciple of Jesus, who has already had a taste of kingdom living in the messianic community, to pray "thy kingdom come": both now, as it has been inaugurated by Jesus among men, and finally, in the last great day of fulfillment. The kingdom of God is at one and the same time, a present reality and a future hope. This petition expresses concern for the fullest possible realization of this kingdom within human history, as well as its final coming in all of its glorious fullness.

*Thy will be done, on earth as it is in heaven* (10b). Of course the will of God is the establishment of His kingdom in which the life that Jesus has revealed is most fully realized. This petition expresses the hope that humankind will at last live up to God's intention for it. This divine intention had been perceived, albeit indistinctly, in the law of the covenant; it had been glimpsed, sometimes faintly, in the proclamation of the prophets; and now it was being revealed with crystal clarity by Jesus. The messianic community prays for grace to obey the will of God, but its prayer is not limited to itself. It is concerned that the will of God be known and obeyed among all mankind, "on earth as it is in heaven."

In reality, this is a daring request. Only that community which is certain that it has received in Jesus Christ the definitive revelation of the will of God, and is conscious of the fact that this will has become reality in the kingdom inaugurated by Jesus in their midst, will dare to pray in this way. To pray in this way is to say, "May you soon be obeyed by all mankind in the same way in which you are obeyed in heaven." And this is not an exercise in theological speculation in which the community dedicates itself to imagining how life in heaven will be. This prayer grows out of the clear conviction that the life of the kingdom which has already been inaugurated in Jesus is a faithful revelation of God's will in heaven.

*Give us this day our daily bread* (11). In this petition Jesus expresses concern for human existence which is temporal and precarious. The first person plural pronouns (we, us, our) occur eight times in the brief space of three verses (11-13). They refer to the messianic community which has grown up around Jesus and depends on the provident grace of God for its very life. The persistent conviction has endured throughout the history of God's people that humankind truly depends on what God gives to sustain its life, for its well-being, for its blessedness, for its salvation. Yahweh is the One who "executes justice for the oppressed; who gives food to the hungry" (Psalm 146:7). The words "this day" in this petition underline the same idea of God's providence. Fragile creatures depend daily on the gracious providence of God. This does not mean that people are therefore simply victims of circumstance from one day to another in a totally arbitrary way. The people of God know by experience that God is faithful "to all generations" and therefore they confront the future with confidence (Psalm 89:1).

The "bread" of this petition is material bread. It provides the nutrients necessary to sustain human life (Psalm 104:15). Before long in its history, the church began to give this "bread" a spiritual interpretation. The Christian church has generally found it relatively easy to trust in God for the salvation of the soul. But to really trust in God for survival in a hostile world has not come easily. However, in the context of the Lord's Prayer, this bread is real. To live and to serve God, persons must depend on the sustenance which God gives for the body. The plural form of this petition (as is the case of the two that follow) points to the communitarian context in which God's gifts are received. Although bread is necessary to sustain the life of each individual, its sufficient provision is reason for the concern and, therefore the petition, *of* the community *in behalf of* the entire community. The selfish consumption of the fruits of the earth is entirely incompatible with the nature of the life which is shared in the messianic community.

*And forgive us our debts, as we also have forgiven our debtors* (12). In the same way in which the forgiveness of God is experienced in the messianic community, so also there is a mutual forgiveness of indebtedness. On occasions the text found in Ephesians 4:32—"And be kind to one another, tenderhearted, forgiving one another, as God in Christ forgave you"—is pitted against this petition in the Lord's Prayer. It is alleged that the Ephesians passage describes a relationship of grace, whereas the text from the Lord's Prayer presents a legalistic obligation. This interpretation, of course, fails to recognize the essential gospel character of the Sermon on the Mount. While it is true that "as we also have forgiven our debtors" is in the past tense, the parallel in the Lukan version (11:4) is in the present tense. And, in neither of these passages is the forgiveness of personal indebtedness presented as a condition which obliges God to be merciful toward humankind. In reality, they offer a description of the situation which prevails in the messianic community. Divine forgiveness is authentically experienced in that particular human community in which personal indebtedness, as well as offenses, are freely forgiven.

The Greek terms translated "debts" and "debtors" in this text, as well as in the rest of the New Testament, carry the meaning of debt and debtor in a literal sense (Romans 4:4; Matthew 18:24; 18:32). Generally their meaning in this text has been understood in religious terms, as offenses and offenders in a more strictly spiritual sense. However, this use of language would seem to indicate that there is an especially close relationship in the messianic community between mutual forgiveness of personal indebtedness and divine forgiveness which is so fundamental. In the version of the Lord's Prayer which Luke offers, the meaning of this relationship appears even more clearly. "And forgive us our sins, for we ourselves forgive every one who is indebted to us" (11:4). The present tense of the verb in the second phrase, "forgive," in reality implies that the messianic community is accustomed to forgiving indebtedness.

Immediately following the Lord's Prayer, Matthew adds two verses (14, 15) in which Jesus offers additional comments about the meaning of this petition. The Greek term translated "forgive" in these two verses is the same verb which is used in verse 12. However, instead of using the term "debts," as he had done in verse 12, Jesus now uses another word which is translated "trespasses," or "offenses" (14, 15). In this way Matthew makes the point that it is *also* necessary to forgive the offenses of other persons if we expect to really experience divine forgiveness for our offenses. In effect, what Jesus had said about "debts" (12) also applies to "offenses" (14, 15). Therefore, this passage really deals with two different, but related questions: the forgiveness of indebtedness and the pardon of offenses.

A prominent aspect of the new messianic era was to be the forgiveness of indebtedness according to the provisions of the Jubilee (Luke 4:18, 19; Isaiah 61:1, 2; Leviticus 26; Deuteronomy 15). But the messianic community is also the sphere in which forgiveness of offenses is experienced. It is here that we are forgiven and we forgive (Matthew 18:15-20; *et al.*). This fundamental relationship between forgiving and receiving forgiveness is emphasized in the New Testament. At least six times it is repeated that willingness to forgive somehow bears a direct relationship to being forgiven (Matthew 6:12; 6:14, 15; 18:35; Mark 11:25; Ephesians 4:32; Colossians 3:13). In the same way in which we have experienced divine forgiveness, we also freely forgive one another in the messianic community inaugurated by Jesus. By the grace of God, participation in the kingdom which Jesus brought is to participate in a community of forgiveness.

*And lead us not into temptation, but deliver us from [the] evil [one]* (13a). The community which is gathered by the Messiah depends on the heavenly Father for its bread, for forgiveness and, finally, for liberation. The verb which is here translated "lead" also means to "guide" or to "lead into." This term expresses the Old Testament conviction that it was Yahweh who guided His people and led them into the Promised Land. In the Old Testament, Yahweh is also depicted as the shepherd who leads His sheep. In its best moments, Israel did not want to be left alone to choose its own paths independently of Yahweh. They looked to God to lead them.

Our version of this passage, "lead us not into temptation," can give the impression that God is somehow responsible for the temptations which besiege us. But this implication is unfortunate. James 1:13, 14 declares clearly that God does not incite us to evil. The temptation to do wrong proceeds from another source. This petition apparently expresses the hope of the community that God will sustain them in the hour of testing.

The "temptation" mentioned in this petition is apparently some sort of diabolical ruse aimed at diverting God's people from their true purpose. The ultimate source of this temptation is the evil one. The Greek term translated in the RSV by "evil" in this petition of the Lord's Prayer is used in several ways in Matthew's Gospel. It may refer to that which is bad, or evil, or malevolent (5:11; 6:23; *et al.*), or to a violent or an evil person (5:39, 45; 7:11;

*et al.*), or to the devil (5:37; 13:19, 38). While these three mean-ings are not mutually exclusive and remind us of the diabolical diversity of evil, the third is certainly fundamental. For this reason some versions of the New Testament translate this petition, "but save us from the evil one" (e.g., *The New English Bible* and *The Jerusalem Bible*).

The liberation to which the messianic community aspires is to be delivered from the control of these "powers" which manifest themselves in so many different ways. The community of the Messiah lives in the confidence that God will finally lead them into the "promised land" of the coming kingdom. Therefore, despite the community's engagement in constant conflict with evil in all of its manifold forms, they are sustained by hope, a hope which illumines the future based on God's faithfulness in the past and the present.

God frees His people in order to love and to serve. When this freedom is abused in unjust relationships toward others, this means quite simply that we have totally misunderstood the true nature of God and His liberation. Jesus gives a graphic example of this kind of misunderstanding in the parable of the two debtors (Matthew 18:23-35).

*For thine is the kingdom and the power and the glory, for ever. Amen* (13b). This doxology with which the Lord's Prayer ends does not appear in many of the more recent versions of the New Testament. Apparently it is not found in the oldest (and therefore most trustworthy) manuscripts of the New Testament. However, it is representative of the kind of liturgical formula with which the messianic community gave expression to its firm con-viction that the kingdom which had been inaugurated by the Messiah bears within it the seeds of power and glory which will one day be revealed in all of their fullness. Meanwhile the glorious form of the future kingdom is already prefigured in the experience of the messianic community.

This eschatological community (eschatological in the sense that it already participates in the life of "the age to come") gives expression to its living hope through the doxologies with which it worships. This doxology is perfectly attuned to the spirit of the New Testament community so it should come as no surprise to find a number of similar doxologies in its pages. The following are only a few examples. "To the only God, our Savior through Jesus Christ our Lord, be glory, majesty, dominion, and authority, before all time and now and for ever. Amen." "To him who sits upon the throne and to the Lamb be blessing and honor and glory and might for ever and ever!" "The kingdom of the world has become the kingdom of our Lord and of his Christ, and he shall reign for ever and ever." (Jude 25; Revelation 5:13; 11:15.)

*Fasting (Matthew 6:16-18)*. We note here again that Jesus, even more clearly than in the case of His instructions on the practices of almsgiving and prayer, is not opposed, in principle, to Jewish piety, but rather to the religious vanity for which it frequently furnished the occasion.

Although fasting is a practice which is common to all the principal religions of the world, there are several unique elements which characterized the practice in ancient Judaism. Their fasting was based on their understanding of the absolute sovereignty of Yahweh. Therefore, fasting prepared the faithful to meet God, not in the sense of a rite of purification which elevates the person to the level of the divine, but rather in the sense of a detached spirit of waiting before the imminent act of God's self-revelation (Exodus 34:28; Deuteronomy 9:9; Daniel 9:3; 10:2-12). Fasting in the Old Testament was also intimately related to the varying fortunes of Israel in its historical existence. It accompanied times of national humiliation and prayer in behalf of Israel's restoration (2 Samuel 12:16-18; 1 Kings 21:27; Psalm 69:11). The most prominent characteristic of the Old Testament concept of fasting is its vision of the practice as an expression of submission to Yahweh. There were also official fasts which were integrated into public worship (Leviticus 16:29-31; 23:27-29, etc.). When fasting was attached to special acts of public worship, it became an occasion for the abuses which were the objects of prophetic denunciation (Isaiah 58:6, 7; Jeremiah 14:12; Joel 2:13; Zechariah 7:5, 6).

In Jesus' time fasting was valued highly as a cultic practice and occupied an important place in Jewish religious life. In addition to the regular fast days, Jews who were especially zealous fasted voluntarily twice a week (on Mondays and Thursdays). In this the Pharisees were especially strict (Luke 18:12). Fasting came to be considered as an especially meritorious and powerful good work with which to please God.

Although the disciples of Jesus apparently continued the ancient Jewish custom of fasting, the presence of the Messiah in the midst of His people served to modify radically the meaning of this practice. (See Matthew 9:14-17; 17:21; Acts 13:3; 14:23; 27:9.) From the perspective of the messianic kingdom which had arrived in Jesus, the practice of fasting, in principle, has been surpassed. However, in light of the interim between the inauguration of the kingdom in the person and work of Jesus the Messiah, and the consummation of the kingdom in the Parousia, there appears to still be a place for fasting "between the times." But the practice of fasting has now been filled with new meaning since the coming of the Messiah. Among other things, it will accompany the practice of the "new righteousness" of the kingdom, responding to the ancient prophetic vision (Isaiah 58:6, 7).

*When you fast, do not look dismal, like the hypocrites* (16). Here again, "hypocrite" can be understood in two different senses: pretending to be sad when one is really not; and in a deeper and more tragic sense, feeling really dismal, and taking advantage of this situation to call people's attention to the fact. In other words, these persons, themselves, are really the victims of their own gloomy piety. In this context (verses 16-18) it seems that the second of these interpretations is the most likely.

The seriousness with which these hypocrites "disfigure their faces" (16) makes them objects of genuine pity. The Greek verb which is here translated "disfigure" means to disfigure to such a degree that the object of disfiguration becomes unrecognizable. In fact the same verb is employed in verse 19 where it is translated "consume." The corrosive effects of rust render treasures unrecognizable. The force of this term "disfigure" is further illustrated by its use in Acts 13:41, where it is translated "perish," and in James 4:14, where it is translated "vanish." Apparently these hypocrites took their fasting with ghastly seriousness or Jesus is employing ironic humor in His description of their appearance.

This disfiguring effect was attained, not merely by means of the grotesque grimaces which made them caricatures of sadness, but also by means of the application of ashes to their faces, an untrimmed and disheveled beard, and a generally dirty and unkempt appearance. Jesus condemned this kind of comportment, not merely because it really didn't contribute to an attitude of true humiliation, but because they did it to call people's attention to their practice of piety (6:1, 5, 16, 18). And in attempting this they were in reality robbing God of the glory which is due Him as sole Judge (6:1). Since it was their intention to make an impression on people, they had already received all the reward that was coming to them. They have received their payment in full.

On the other hand, Jesus tells His disciples that they should not vary their daily habit of cleanliness when they fast. They are urged to "anoint" their heads and "wash" their faces just like they do every other day of their lives. In fact, there is a sense in which all of life, as it is lived in the messianic community, is a fast. Therefore the disciple of Jesus does not need artificial aids, such as a generally disheveled appearance or an ashen face in order to call attention to personal piety. Character and deeds which correspond to the nature of the kingdom will be the distinguishing features of a person's fasting (5:13-16).

The authentic fast, performed before God rather than people, is pleasant to God and Jesus assures His disciples that God will reward them in a way that is fitting, not according to the religious values which are generally held, but according to the values of the kingdom.

Few aspects of the religious life of His time bothered Jesus more than hypocrisy which led persons to pretend a piety which was in reality false, or worse yet, to submit their practice of piety to others of similar religious opinions for their approval, rather than to God, "the Father who sees in secret" (6:4, 6, 18). For this reason Jesus charged the scribes and Pharisees with being "blind guides," "blind fools," "a child of hell," "whitewashed tombs" and "serpents" (Matthew 23).

But we do well to remember that hypocrisy is precisely the temptation which most tantalizes religious people. The various forms with which we give expression to the reality of our spiritual experience are in the beginning authentic. They reflect the reality of our experience as members of the body of Christ. But in the absence of experiences in the life of the people of God which are continually new and vital, the religious forms with which we attempt to express our piety become routine and are eventually hardened into tradition. And the history of the church warns us that tradition, with the passing of years and decades and centuries, becomes more and more sacred. This explains why it becomes so easy to practice our piety for the purpose of keeping up appearances. And our practice of piety becomes a "theatrical production" because it no longer responds to the realities of fresh spiritual experience.

The solution to this problem does not lie in our ability for religious innovation. It is not merely a matter of abandoning the expressions of our piety, our liturgy (service to God), in order to constantly begin anew. Jesus assumed that His disciples would continue these practices which are concrete forms of expressing a relationship with God. But we need to be alert to the subtle dangers which are present. The remedy for the hypocritical ostentation which is described in these passages is the continual cultivation of a fresh and authentic personal relationship with God, offering all of the expressions of our faith to our "Father who sees" (6:4, 6, 18). Under the searchlight of His judgment our practice of piety will be continually renewed and we will constantly experience new dimensions of relationship with God, as well as with our brothers and sisters in the family of God.

### The problem of property (Matthew 6:19-34)

The context in which these teachings of Jesus are set shows us that the problem of property is not merely a question with economic, legal, or social dimensions. It is, in reality, a spiritual matter which deeply affects our relationship with God. Just as in the case of the other ways in which piety is practiced (almsgiving, prayer, and fasting), the forms in which property is acquired and the ways in which these material elements so necessary to sustain human life are used, as well as the inner attitudes we take toward them, are of fundamental importance in determining our relationship to God. In these teachings Jesus proclaims with graphic clarity the exclusive claim which God makes on the life of His people.

The teachings of Jesus in this rather complex section of the Sermon on the Mount can apparently be organized around three specific instructions to His followers: "Do not lay up for yourselves treasures on earth ... but lay up for yourselves treasures in heaven" (6:19a, 20a); "Do not be anxious about your life, what you shall eat or what you shall drink, nor about your body, what you shall put on.... Do not be anxious about tomorrow" (6:25, 34a); "But seek first his kingdom and his righteousness, and all these things shall be yours as well" (6:33).

These instructions are presented in an imperative form and, as commands, they call for decision and appropriate action on the part of Jesus' hearers. The scope of the instructions themselves is broadened and their meaning is illustrated by means of a series of proverbs and popular sayings. These were typical in Jewish literature of the period and were known as "wisdom" sayings. In this way the imagination of the hearers is stimulated and they are carried on to new levels of reflection and understanding and, hopefully, more obedient action. In these proverbs, drawn from Hebrew wisdom literature, the insistent repetition so characteristic of Semitic parallelism and the vivid images drawn from the common experience of the hearers served to make an even stronger impact on the lives of Jesus' disciples.

*Do not lay up for yourselves treasures on earth ... but lay up for yourselves treasures in heaven* (Matthew 6:19a, 20a). The essentially perishable nature of material goods is depicted by the images of "moth," "rust," and "thieves." Garments which were hoarded at home ended up by being eaten by the larvae of moths. The coins and jewels which Palestinian peasants or laborers buried in the ground in periods of political and economic instability were sometimes completely disfigured by the corrosive effects of the humidity and the soil. And when they tried to save them by hiding them in their houses they were often stolen by thieves who easily made holes through the fragile mud bricks.

In contrast, "treasures in heaven" escape the havoc which "treasures on earth" are bound to suffer. But what are these "treasures in heaven"? And how are they laid up? The parallel passage in Luke sheds light on the meaning of the phrase. "Sell your possessions and give alms; provide yourselves ... with a treasure in the heavens that does not fail, where no thief approaches and no moth destroys" (12:33). And there are other passages where the phrase is understood in the same sense. Jesus, for example, said to the rich young ruler, "Sell what you possess and give to the poor, and you will have treasure in heaven" (Matthew 19:21; Mark 10:21; Luke 18:22). And of the rich fool it was said, "So is he who lays up treasure for himself, and is not rich toward God" (Luke 12:21). So it appears that "treasures in heaven" are laid up by means of the practice of generosity toward those who are in need. (See 1 Timothy 6:17-19.) In fact, this is the way in which the phrase "treasures in heaven" was commonly understood among the Jews of Jesus' time. Jesus was talking about something that everyone understood clearly. For Jesus, this insight must have been very important, because practically every time that He had something to say about riches or property He repeated these words, or others which were very similar to these (Matthew 19:21 and parallels; Luke 12:21, 33).

Of course the words of Jesus about the importance of doing one's piety before God and submitting to His judgment alone, rather than doing it to impress people (6:1, 4, 6, 18) are especially fitting here. The generosity which lays up "treasures in heaven" is not practiced before people with a view to being seen and appreciated by them, but with reference to the "Father who sees in secret."

With this teaching (and the corresponding warning) Jesus invites His disciples to be, in fact, a community which is characterized by generosity, where those who possess take the initiative and share with those who do not have what they need. In his call to repentance as preparation to participation in the coming kingdom, John the Baptist had already caught the vision of this communitarian element in that life which characterizes the new messianic order. "He who has two coats, let him share with him who has none; and he who has food, let him do likewise" (Luke 3:11). Although Jesus does not give any concrete definitions about the ways in which this teaching will be implemented in the life of His community, He does develop the principle with force and clarity.

One of the most pressing challenges which faces the Christian church of our time is, undoubtedly, the creation of concrete expressions of brotherhood in the sphere of economics. We need to find forms of living together and sharing which express unequivocally the principle which Jesus taught. The messianic community dare not conform itself to merely reproducing those economic models which characterize our contemporary systems. Rather than merely attempting to humanize existing economic systems, the messianic community dares to be radical in its attempt to give concrete forms to the principles which Jesus enunciated.

At times the church has been tempted to try to solve the economic and social problems which plague society by backing with its authority the imposition of a "just" order by force on a total society. That this constitutes a real temptation to those who are concerned for social justice is easily understandable. However, the church will do well to resist the temptation to use coercive power to attain just ends. On the other hand, the church should surely seek to create models of social and economic sharing which truly reflect the words as well as the spirit of Jesus and demonstrate their viability in its corporate life.

In the verses which follow, Jesus uses three phrases not unlike the biblical proverbs, to lend emphasis and clarity to the principle outlined in verses 19 and 20.

*For where your treasure is, there will your heart be also (21).* Although our version does not reflect the fact, the possessive pronouns, "your," both appear in their singular form. We have already noticed Jesus' approach—first presenting principles in general terms and then applying them personally and directly (by using the singular form) for the benefit of His disciples (see Matthew 5:38-42). This verse reveals an important facet of the biblical concept of person. The heart is attracted by the treasure freely chosen. Every person has a treasure. But no one can have more than one. The treasure which a person chooses in turn exercises an exclusive power over the person. Through this biblical proverb Jesus warns us that the values which we choose for ourselves finally determine our destiny.

*. . .if your eye is sound, your whole body will be full of light; but if your eye is not sound, your whole body will be full of darkness* (22b; 23a). According to Old Testament thought a person's eye is the lamp which permits orientation of one's life, to find the way in the midst of the world's darkness. If a person's eye is sound (literally, "single" or "good"), the orientation will be well accomplished. If, on the other hand, the eye is not sound (literally, "evil"), then the person will be lost in the darkness. The text of Proverbs 22:9 helps us to understand the sense in which Jesus used this proverb: "He who has a bountiful eye will be blessed, for he shares his bread with the poor." In a more literal sense the first line of the proverb could be translated "he who has a *good* eye will be blessed." In any case, the sense of Jesus' teaching here is clear. A person whose life is characterized by generosity and deeds of mercy lives in the light. On the other hand, in the Semitic languages "evil eye" means avaricious or miserly. A person who is characterized by avarice and selfishness will find his life invaded by the darkness which surrounds him.

*No one can serve two masters; for either he will hate the one and love the other, or he will be devoted to the one and despise the other. You cannot serve God and mammon (24).*

These words, taken within their context here, show the truly radical character of Jesus' teachings in relation to riches and property. Material possessions become a false god who demands the same loyalty from a person as God requires of him. For this reason the demands which material possessions are capable of imposing upon a person must be rejected outright.

Judging from its form, this verse appears to be a Semitic proverb in which the main idea is spoken in the first line and developed and deepened in successive lines. In this way Jesus underscores what He has already said about the fundamental human nature: persons will always place themselves and their services at the disposal of someone or something. To imagine that one is totally free to determine self-destiny, and therefore is servant to no one appears to be utterly pretentious. To imagine that it is possible to serve two masters is to indulge in a groundless illusion.

The term "to belong to" probably offers a better translation of the biblical idea of service reflected in verse 24. It is not merely a matter of rendering some service, but rather the kind of total availability which a master could expect of his slave. This verse reflects the kind of relationship which excludes all other loyalties. To "hate" (line 1) means to separate oneself in total indifference from someone. To "love" in this context carries the opposite connotation. It means to belong to another, and to serve that person with one's whole being. To "be devoted to" (line 2) translates a term which means to attach oneself to another. To "despise" means the opposite, to dissociate oneself from another.

In the last line of verse 24 Jesus offers a succinct and powerful résumé of His teaching on this subject. A person serves God by means of concrete expressions of unselfish and self-giving love toward one's fellows. And this, by the nature of things, is the way in which a person lays up treasures in heaven. On the other hand, a person serves mammon (and according to Jesus it is impossible to serve another simultaneously) by orienting one's life and affections in material values. Jesus calls this way of living "laying up treasures on earth." Mammon is the Aramaic term for "profits." This accounts for the fact that in some English versions the term is translated "money." Mammon is used especially in the sense of

having an evil power or debasing influence such as that exercised
by a false god.

Although this teaching of Jesus does not constitute a denial
of the validity of those material goods which are so necessary for
the support of human life, His words do cut very deeply and they
place before us a bewildering dilemma. To what degree is it possible for us to possess properties and money without allowing
ourselves to fall into their possession? The messianic community is
called to find ways to resist the temptation to "love" them, to "be
devoted" to them, to "serve" them.

*Do not be anxious about your life, what you shall eat or what
you shall drink, nor about your body, what you shall put on* . . . .
*Do not be anxious about tomorrow* (6:25, 34a).

Here again Jesus identifies a principle: it is a contradiction to
be anxious about one's life in the messianic community (25a). In
the following verses He describes more fully what He means by
this anxiety about life. Concretely, it includes the question of
food, drink, clothing, and a secure future. Here, too, the implications of this principle are clarified, illustrated, and broadened by
means of another series of Semitic proverbs and popular wisdom
sayings in order that Jesus' listeners might understand well what
He had in mind in this teaching.

Six times within the limits of these ten verses (25-34) Jesus
repeats a term which is translated in our version by the phrase "be
anxious." Jesus is here referring to that kind of anxiety which leads
to a divided loyalty and, then, to an idolatrous concentration on
material possessions.

The New Testament recognizes that human existence is
characterized by struggle, solicitude, and concern. The abundance of warnings against being anxious (Matthew 6:25-34;
Philippians 4:6; 1 Peter 5:7) take human nature as their point of
reference—everybody tends to be anxious in one way or another.
Those who participate in the messianic community will engage in
productive work like other persons. But they will do so free of
worry and anxiety because as persons who already belong to God's
kingdom, its values are determinative in all that happens in their

lives. So their "concerns" will not exceed what is necessary in order to provide for material sustenance of their brothers and sisters, as well as their own (Ephesians 4:28).

Anxiety is, in reality, a pagan characteristic (6:7, 32). They do not realize that there is a "Father [who] knows what you need" (6:8). In the messianic community the uncertainties of life do not cause anxiety because its members know, by experience as well as by faith, that the future, as well as the present, are in God's hands. For this reason the apostle counsels his fellow disciples to "cast all your anxieties on him, for he cares about you" (1 Peter 5:7; cf. Philippians 4:6). The remedy which Jesus offers for anxiety is confidence in God in the context of the community of the kingdom. In the verses that follow Jesus underscores this fact with four illustrations.

*Is not life more than food, and the body more than clothing?* (25b). Since God's children, who have been created in His image as living beings, are worth infinitely more than the nutrients which sustain them and the clothing with which their bodies are covered, we may confidently trust in the providence of God to sustain and to protect those whom He has created. God can be counted on to care about our food and clothing, since He after all concerns Himself about our very lives.

*Look at the birds of the air ... the lilies of the field ... the grass of the field* (26, 28, 30). Of course birds struggle for their survival. But in and of themselves they would be incapable of providing for their sustenance. God provides for them far beyond their own efforts. The purpose of this illustration is to show that if God looks after the birds, and indeed He does, how much more will He care for man. And if the Creator crowns with so much beauty the flowers and the grass of the fields which flourish for only a day, He can surely be counted on to look after the children of His own family.

*And which of you by being anxious can add one cubit to his span of life?* (27). Human anxieties, and even those concerns which might be considered to be legitimate, show us that there are insurmountable limits to what we are capable of attaining.

God alone is able to cause the body to grow taller or one's life-span to be extended. In the face of these limitations human anxiety seems all the more foolish. The accumulation of material possessions will not even serve to prolong the life of the anxious possessor one cubit more.

*Let the day's own trouble be sufficient for the day* (34). Confident trust in God, as Father, and an all-consuming search for the kingdom are the things which free a person from the anxieties of an unknown future. Furthermore, in the face of today's troubles it is doubly foolish to waste time and energies worrying about tomorrow.

Of course our economic structures are different from the ones which prevailed in first-century Palestine. We have come to call "insurance" and "savings" that which Jesus, in His time, called anxious concern about tomorrow. The usury which was forbidden in the Gospels has come to be considered legitimate and is called "charging interest." But be this as it may, Jesus has here offered some principles which we dare not disregard without grave risk to our spiritual well-being. When savings begin to accumulate and investments grow disproportionately and interest charges become an excessive burden for a brother in need, then these warnings of Jesus must be taken seriously.

*But seek first his kingdom and his righteousness, and all these things shall be yours as well* (6:33). In this instruction Jesus summarizes His teaching about property, material possessions, and money. Anxiety grows out of a scale of values which is really pagan in its essence. One who knows no other way to assure his future than by means of accumulating material possessions is, in reality, condemning himself to an anxious existence. On the other hand, followers of Jesus have an all-consuming cause to which they are dedicated—the kingdom of God and His righteousness.

The solution to the oppressive pagan anxiety which characterizes people in our time is found in the messianic kingdom. The person who seeks security in property, in possessions, and in fiscal solvency stands condemned to a life of anxiety. But one who begins by seeking the kingdom of God finds freedom from anxieties in the providence of God who both sustains that life and provides for all the person's needs.

It is clear from this summary statement that Jesus is not proposing the kind of passive and resigned trust in providence which has sometimes characterized Oriental thought and practice. Neither does He suggest a sort of mystical contempt for the physical body and its needs in contrast to the soul and a person's spiritual needs. Nor does He teach a naive optimism which refuses to take seriously the harsh realities of human existence on this earth. Instead, He calls on persons to look for that which is of real value, "the kingdom of God and his righteousness." The kingdom of God which has been inaugurated by the Messiah is, in its essence, a kingdom of righteousness, or justice (see Romans 14:17). There is a fundamental relationship between the cause of Christ and "righteousness' sake," or the cause of justice, (Matthew 5:10, 11). The righteousness of the kingdom is God's gift which makes it possible for persons to live together in harmonious and just relationships as God has intended for His people. In the messianic community a personally satisfying simplification of life becomes a possibility. Material goods are administered in line with God's purposes and there are resources to provide for those in need. The absolute loyalty of this community to God frees its members from the anxieties which an oppressive materialistic orientation produces. In the community of the kingdom, life is shared in the spirit of Jesus Christ.

This understanding of the place of material goods in human society is radical and revolutionary. There is a widespread tendency among persons to think of themselves and their own needs first and then to think of others. Jesus asks the opposite of His followers. He invites persons to enter His community of love which prefigures the kingdom of God which will one day be revealed in all its splendor. Here life, including material possessions, is shared and provision is made for all of a person's needs. One catches a glimpse of the way in which this promise is fulfilled in Mark 10:29, 30 and its parallels: "Truly, I say to you, there is no one who has left house or brothers or sisters or mother or father or children or lands, for my sake and for the gospel, who will not receive a hundredfold now in this time, houses and brothers and sisters and mothers and children and lands, with persecutions, and in the age to come eternal life."

To those who leave everything in order to follow Him, Jesus promises a community in which the necessities of life are shared. We need not wait until the end of time to see this promise fulfilled, because Jesus offers it now, with the promise of His presence in meeting persecution. Jesus invites His disciples to enter into that community which is characterized by its family spirit, where no one lives for self alone, where any person who has had to leave biological family or material possessions for the sake of Christ will find both family and goods among the brothers and sisters in God's family. The material needs of Jesus' disciples will be provided by their Father who works through His generous community.

In reality, this is the same spirit which we find reflected in the primitive community in Jerusalem (Acts 2:43-47; 4:32-37), in the various Christian communities to which Paul's letters were directed (Romans 12:13; Ephesians 4:28), as well as John's (1 John 3:16-18) and James's (2:15-17). Throughout the later history of the church this spirit has manifested itself time and again, and the economic practices of the community have taken on fraternal dimensions whenever men and women have been touched anew by the living Spirit of God and have taken seriously these teachings of Jesus.

There is a parallelism in the Sermon on the Mount which has often gone unnoticed. There is an evident relationship between the attitude which Jesus took toward violence (5:38-48) and His attitude toward wealth (6:18-34). It should be pointed out, in passing, that Paul also shared this same double concern, as we note by the way in which he deals with these two themes in juxtaposition in Romans 12:13, 14.

However, the Christian church (and it is surely no mere coincidence) has tended to play down the radicality of both of these teachings. Although Jesus said that it would be extremely difficult for a rich man to enter the kingdom of heaven (Matthew 19:23, 24; Mark 10:24, 25; Luke 18:24, 25), the church has generally gone out of its way to make their entrance easier, and even congratulates itself for the rich and the powerful who appear on its membership roles. Although Jesus and the apostles warn of the grave dangers which property and wealth occasion to the people of God (1 Timothy 6:10, 17-19; James 4:13—5:6), the church, on the other hand, has generally attempted to enhance its position in society by strengthening its economic and institutional base, either through its own financial solvency or through that of its members. In fact, among individual Christians financial solvency and economic power have sometimes been considered signs of God's pleasure and as rewards for virtue rather than dangers and sources of temptation.

The Christian church has treated Jesus' teachings concerning vengeance and violence in a similar way. The radicality of Jesus' instructions has been softened so that only "legitimate" vengeance is exacted and only "justifiable" violence is employed. In fact the church has often purchased its security by allying itself with secular power rather than taking the hazardous path of peacemaking and self-giving love. Christians have generally felt justified in defending their rights through the violence of self-defense and litigation instead of opting for the precariousness which the kind of vulnerability which Jesus practiced and taught to His disciples implies. In fact, the use of violence in the interests of so-called "just" causes is generally considered to be a virtue among Christians.

However, we need to ask ourselves, why not take both of these teachings with equal seriousness? In reality, both carry the stamp of Jesus' own authority. Both nonresistance and detachment from material possessions, when they are really put into practice, require the grace and providence of God for survival. In fact, sharing goods, as well as renouncing all recourse to violence in social relationships, are humanly hazardous steps of confident trust in God in the kind of violent and materialistic society in which we live.

## Questions for Discussion

1. Do you agree with the statement that hypocrisy is the besetting sin of religious people and anxiety is fundamentally a problem for nonbelievers? What does this tell us in the light of our anxieties?

2. Has it ever occurred to you that aspects of your worship might be more to keep up appearances than as authentic expressions of spiritual relationship? If so, in what direction do solutions lie?

3. In all probability you know few, if any, full-fledged hypocrites who maliciously pretend to be what they are not. But do you know any "innocent" or "sincere" hypocrites who, although well intentioned, are obviously deceiving themselves in their religiosity? What is the remedy for their plight?

4. In our practice of prayer we can easily fall into the trap of formalism. What are some biblical secrets for keeping prayer vital?

5. Is there a direct relationship between being willing to forgive economic indebtedness and being disposed to receive God's forgiveness? Or should "debts" and "debtors" in the Lord's Prayer be understood in a strictly spiritual sense?

6. Do you feel that fasting has any place in the messianic community? What might be some specific applications of this practice in our time?

7. Do you agree that treating the problem of property in the context of the theme of true spirituality is intentional? If so, how do economic matters concretely affect both our vertical and horizontal spiritual relationships?

8. What implications do Jesus' teachings about possessions have for "rich Christians in an age of hunger"?

9. Can you think of concrete steps which you might take in your congregation to express more fully the biblical reality of brotherhood in the economic sphere?

10. It is sometimes argued that Jesus' economic teachings are impractical for our time. Would it make any difference if we approached the question from the perspective of a sharing community of disciples rather than as individual Christians?

11. Persons who live in Christian communities in which economic resources are freely shared for the needs of all report that the experience is truly liberating. What has been your experience? Are you free? Or are you tempted to be "anxious" about your future security?

12. What are the missionary implications of being a rich and powerful church? What would be the implications of being a poor and weak church? Do the concrete conditions of the incarnation speak to this question?

# Chapter 7

# Instructions and Warnings for Life in the Kingdom (Matthew 7:1-27)

The first two chapters of the Sermon on the Mount describe the character of the human community which is gathered by the Messiah in anticipation of the kingdom of God which will, one day, appear in all of its glory. First of all, we are given a brief description of the citizens of this community. They are humble, they have deep social concerns, and they are nonviolent. They are moved to action by their concern for justice in human relationships. They are characterized by a spirit of forgiveness, generosity, sincerity, and peace. And precisely because they have chosen to order their lives according to the values of the coming kingdom, they suffer under the persecution of the powers which control this present "evil age" (5:3-16).

Next, we are given a number of glimpses at what it means to live together in this messianic community. It is a family in which interpersonal relationships are uncorrupted by hurtful expressions of anger or desire for vengeance. The basic concern for the well-being of others serves to guard its members against marital infidelity as well as against all forms of unfaithfulness. It is a community in which the truth is communicated in love. In fact, God's love is such a powerful force in its midst that violent men are unable to destroy it by persecution (5:17-48).

Finally the relationships of the subjects in the kingdom to their Lord and King are described. Their personal relationship with God frees them from the temptation to practice their piety for reasons of ostentation. The life of this community is sustained by sincere confidence in their Father and nurtured by prayer. It is a community in which the idolatrous tyranny of material possessions and wealth has been conquered through a life of authentic sharing in the Spirit (6:1-34).

The community which the Sermon on the Mount describes is not a utopia, a beautiful vision which is never realized. It is a family of men and women who respond to the Messiah's invitation to begin to experience, by the grace of God, the life which corresponds to the kingdom. Of course in relation to the rest of human society this kind of community is forced to live against the current. This is the context in which we can understand Jesus' teachings contained in the last chapter of the Sermon on the Mount. In order to protect it against the dangers which threaten its life, and in order to conserve the different quality of life which characterizes His community, Jesus offers a series of instructions and warnings. There are instructions related to the problems which confront the community and warnings against those dangers which are considered to be even more serious and threaten the community's very life.

### Instructions and admonitions (Matthew 7:1-12)

*Judge not.* The first instruction (7:1-5) deals with the process of discernment and restoration, or the experience of forgiveness in the community, and is synthesized in its most concise form in its counsel: "Judge not, that you be not judged" (1). This instruction clearly has to do with life as it is lived in the Christian community. Three times we find the word "brother" repeated in this section (3, 4, 5). Here Jesus is dealing with the problem which occurs in a community whose moral standards are high. The ethical zeal of its members can easily lead to attitudes of moral and spiritual superiority on the part of some. Motivated by what they erroneously believe to be a high degree of responsibility before God and their fellowmen, these persons begin to criticize, to pass judgment, and even to condemn their brothers and sisters for their faults.

Of course the relationship of verses 1 to 5 to Matthew 18:15-20, where we find the same emphasis upon one's relationship to "the brother," will be readily evident. In fact, Matthew 18 provides us with a number of clues for the interpretation of this text. "Binding and loosing" includes the process of moral discernment in the messianic community whereby God's will for the life of His people is known and acknowledged. And this, of course, is a prerequisite for meaningful repentance, restoration, and forgiveness. This process, in turn, is carried out in the context of a loving, mutually responsible, repentant community. In a community characterized by these relationships of mutuality and fraternal concern, attitudes of self-righteousness are clearly out of place. Only those who are truly repentant can restore the erring brother.

Sometimes the counsel "judge not" has been taken in an absolute sense, as a prohibition of all intervention in the problems of a brother. The problem with this interpretation is that it overlooks the teaching in verse 5 with which Jesus concludes this particular instruction. Jesus does not intend to forbid expressions of mutual concern within the community. He does, however, insist that discipline be restorative in its purpose and character. The verb here translated "judge" does not mean merely to form an opinion about the brother's action or to evaluate what he does. It means, rather, to pass judgment definitely or to condemn. The parallel passage in Luke's Gospel makes the meaning of this verse clear: "Judge not, and you will not be judged; condemn not, and you will not be condemned; forgive, and you will be forgiven" (6:37). Jesus does not forbid all appraisal of a brother's actions. However, He does prohibit passing definitive and condemnatory judgments on him, since this prerogative belongs to God alone.

*For with the judgment you pronounce you will be judged, and the measure you give will be the measure you get* (2) serves to deepen and to amplify the meaning of verse 1. The meaning of these two verses seems to be the following: "If you take it upon yourself to condemn your brother or sister, you are really excluding yourself from God's forgiveness." So it is really not a question of being well disposed toward one's brother, or of closing one's eyes to their weaknesses, or of being willing to overlook their sins. It is rather a matter of moral discernment in the context of the Christian community, thoroughgoing repentance, and genuine forgiveness. The parable of the two debtors (Matthew 18:23-35) provides an excellent illustration of the meaning of these verses. The conclusion which Jesus adds to the parable is this: "So also my heavenly Father will do to every one of you, if you do not forgive your brother from your heart" (18:35). We dare not underestimate the importance of being willing to forgive our brother. In fact, our own forgiveness somehow depends upon it. This is so important that it is repeated six more times in the New Testament (Matthew 6:12; 6:14, 15; 18:35; Mark 11:25; Ephesians 4:32; Colossians 3:13). The alternative to passing judgment on one's brother, or condemning him, is not indifference, but restoration through discernment, repentance, and forgiveness. Jesus expects that His disciples will forgive one another in exactly the same way in which God is willing to forgive.

. . .*first take the log out of your own eye.* Verses 3-5 underscore the importance of exercising mutual discipline in the messianic community, but we are warned of possible deformations in the process. Although this fact is not evident in our English translation, the pronouns "you" and "your" in verses 3-5 are all singular. This implies that while the principle is applicable to all, the example cited in these verses has special implications for individual disciples of Jesus. By using the singular form of "you," Jesus personalizes the example and makes specific the identify of the person with "the log" in his eye. *It is I!*

We dare not condemn our brother, but restore him in a spirit of true humility. The example of the "speck" and the "log" suggests, among other things, that only a person who has experienced repentance and forgiveness (from whose eye a log has been removed) is in condition to help his brother with his problem (remove the speck from the eye of the brother); and, in order to live up to our best intentions as disciples of Jesus, we need the help of our brothers and sisters. Our defensive mechanisms do not even allow us to see our own defects, let alone correct them.

This instruction coincides perfectly with other New Testament teachings concerning forgiveness in the church (Matthew 18:15-17; Galatians 6:1, 2; Luke 17:3). From the elements contained in all of these passages a number of fundamental conclusions can be drawn:

The path to restoration and forgiveness is always personal and requires a spirit of genuine humility. The reconciliation of an erring brother or sister requires that someone in the community show concern for them. The removal of a "speck" from someone else's eye is a very delicate procedure and requires an abundance of tender loving care.

In keeping with the communitarian nature of the church, everybody within the brotherhood shares in the responsibility for the restoration of the erring one. It is our concern for our brother's welfare which moves us to come to his aid.

·In line with the fundamental nature of God's mission in the world, a sincere desire for the restoration and reconciliation of the offending person is the only really legitimate motive for the exercise of discipline in the messianic community. Although there may well be other concerns, these will always be secondary to the central interest for the well-being of the person in experiencing genuine forgiveness and restoration.

*Pearls to swine (7:6).* The terminology of this verse provokes our sensibilities and seems a bit distasteful, but it would not have appeared this way to Jesus' hearers. Proverbs of this type were common among the popular sayings in the ancient Near East.

> *"Do not give dogs what is holy;*
> *[Lest] they turn and attack you.*
> *And do not throw your pearls before swine,*
> *Lest they trample them under foot.*°

---

°The literary structure of the verse is poetic and its meaning seems to be more clear if we rearrange the order of the lines in the stanza.

This verse apparently refers to the relationship between members of the messianic community and those outside the community who are either indifferent to its message, or are violently opposed to those who participate in it. In the face of this decided and even violent opposition, caution is counseled. It is not advisable to insist on the implementation of the style of life which corresponds to the values of the kingdom among those who show absolutely no interest in the gospel of the kingdom.

This does not mean that the disciple of Jesus will take the initiative and break all contacts with those who are indifferent and even enemies of the kingdom. Quite to the contrary, the disciple will seek to relate in a redemptive way to these persons. The disciple will not interrupt witness to the Messiah and the kingdom which He has inaugurated, even though it may bring persecution. But in the execution of this mission the messenger will not begin by insisting on the full scope of kingdom ethics (as it is summarized in the Sermon on the Mount) among those who refuse to declare their allegiance to the Lord of the kingdom and who, therefore, do not count on the spiritual resources He gives in order to live in the community of a new era.

Participation in this community presupposes a commitment freely made by the disciple in response to the good news of God's grace. It must be remembered that the ethic of the kingdom is for disciples. The best form of attracting persons to Jesus is by living as Jesus' disciples, by incarnating the values described in the Sermon on the Mount. Insofar as the principles and teachings of the Sermon on the Mount become a part of us, the world will come to know what it means to be a disciple of Jesus.

Jesus' followers undoubtedly understood that they were "not to give . . . what is holy," that is, the values of the kingdom which reflect the very nature of God, nor their "pearls," that is the community's most precious possession, the gospel of Christ, to "dogs" and to "swine," that is, to persons who show an absolute lack of interest in the gospel of the kingdom and who oppose its messengers with violence. But they sought to live the life of the kingdom in the midst of the uninterested in spite of the suffering and persecution that it brought them, just as Jesus had done.

*Ask ... seek ... knock* (7:7-11). At first impression, the third instruction appears to be a continuation of Jesus' earlier teaching on prayer (6:5-15). However, according to verse 11, which is the conclusion toward which the paragraph points, the emphasis does not fall so much on the practice of prayer, as it does on the fact that "even more will your Father who is in heaven give *good things* to those who ask him!" (11). In the version of this teaching which Luke offers, Jesus declares exactly what this "good thing" is: "How much more will the heavenly Father give the *Holy Spirit* to those who ask him!" (11:13).

To live a life based on the values described in the Sermon on the Mount requires infinitely more than the best of human efforts. In order to live the life of the kingdom, the Spirit of the Lord of the kingdom is needed. This is the same Spirit who descended upon Jesus at His baptism enabling Him to fulfill His messianic mission (Mark 1:10, 11; Matthew 3:16, 17). In the new messianic era inaugurated by Jesus, God Himself intervenes in the person of His Spirit to enable and to purify those who participate in His kingdom.

One cannot read the Sermon on the Mount with integrity without feeling humanly powerless and thoroughly prostrated by its requirements. Purely human resources are totally inadequate in the face of its demands. To this sense of human incapacity and frustration Jesus responds, "Ask ... seek ... knock" (7), and the Father will give you His Spirit. This was precisely the prophetic vision of the messianic era. "A new heart I will give you, and a new spirit I will put within you; and I will take out of your flesh the heart of stone and give you a heart of flesh. And I will put my Spirit within you, and cause you to walk in my statutes and be careful to observe my ordinances" (Ezekiel 36:26, 27; Jeremiah 31:33, 34; Joel 2:28, 29).

Beside calling for a style of life based on new values, and a radically new approach, humanity also needs a new knowledge of God, a new experience, a new Spirit, the Spirit of God. The follower of Jesus will find it both worthless and frustrating to attempt to live the values of the Sermon on the Mount without first receiving God's Holy Spirit. But it is the privilege of every Christian to experience the daily presence and power of the Holy Spirit, the continuing presence of Jesus. The presence of the Holy Spirit is none other than the spiritual presence of Jesus. This is the way in which Paul summarizes the mystery of the new life in the body of Christ. "But you are not in the flesh, you are in the Spirit, if in fact the Spirit of God dwells in you. Any one who does not have the Spirit of Christ does not belong to him. . . . For all who are led by the Spirit of God are sons of God" (Romans 8:9, 14). So the Christian life is not merely a question of understanding the will of God and keeping His commandments. It is also communion in the Holy Spirit who makes all of this possible.

The theme of seeking and subsequently finding is prominent in the biblical tradition. Its source is to be found in the writings of the great prophets of Israel. "You will seek me and find me; when you seek me with all your heart, I will be found by you, says the Lord" (Jeremiah 29:13, 14a; see also Matthew 21:21, 22; Luke 17:5, 6; John 14:13, 14; 15:7; 16:23; James 1:5). Although humankind can and should ask and seek, he will receive and find, not because of the intensity of petition or search, but because God in His mercy allows Himself to be found by those who seek. In reality, it is God in His grace, who comes to the seeker. The New Testament teaches us that all can ask and seek and knock in complete confidence because God has revealed Himself in Jesus the Messiah.

The verbs "ask ... seek ... knock" are really parallel synonymous expressions which describe human activity. They are not magical formulas designed to exert pressure on God, but rather promises directed to those who seek with all their heart, that is, in the totality of their being (Jeremiah 29:13). It is possible to state categorically that "every one who asks receives, and he who seeks finds, and to him who knocks it will be opened" (7:8), not because of human insistence, but because of the merciful activity of God who responds, who allows Himself to be found and who hastens to open.

The illustration which Jesus offers in the following two verses (9, 10) points out the fact that a human father who acts as a father should, can be counted on to provide daily food (bread and fish) for his children. In His application, Jesus shows that if these fathers, who humanly speaking are good, but in reality are wayward and fallen, can be counted on to give good things to their children, how much more reasonable it is to expect that the heavenly Father, who is totally different from even the best of earthly fathers, "will give good things to those who ask him" (11). And among these "good things," the greatest and the best is the Holy Spirit (Luke 11:13).

*Do so to them* (7:12). Jesus' fourth instruction is commonly known as the "golden rule." Apparently the idea expressed in this verse was not original with Jesus. It was found, in its negative form at least, among the followers of Confucius, the Greek Stoics, and in Jewish rabbinic literature. (The version attributed to the Jewish rabbi, Hillel, went something like this: "Whatever displeases you, don't do it to another. This is the whole Law; and the rest is commentary.")

But it seems that Jesus was the first to give this saying its positive form. In this instruction Jesus insists on what His disciples should do, without mentioning rewards. The disciples' personal desires guide them in anticipating the needs of others and in reacting to them. Therefore it serves as an instrument which helps them to overcome their own inclinations to self-interest. Potential self-centeredness is turned out toward others. The plural form of this instruction ("you" in this verse is plural) indicates that the point of reference is not the self-centered individual, but rather the messianic community in which persons seek the well-being of others, not merely to avoid having others treat them badly, but because Jesus proceeds this way and this is the nature of relationships in His community. The golden rule in reality serves to broaden the scope of the Sermon on the Mount. As a description of the total comportment of Jesus' disciples, the Sermon on the Mount would be an incomplete document. Jesus did not really intend to touch every situation which arises in the life of His disciples. But it is sufficiently inclusive and specific to describe with clarity the form and the direction which the life of the Christian disciple will take. The golden rule offers a principle which covers situations which are not specifically dealt with in the Sermon on the Mount.

In this verse Jesus asks His disciples to place their love for themselves (and it is generally recognized that this plays an important role in all of us) at the service of their contemporaries. In our interpersonal relationships we should be as sensitive to the needs of others as we are to our own needs.

This verse does not teach us that we should do good to others in order that they will reciprocate with kindness. On the contrary, we are called upon to do for others what we would desire for ourselves. The motivating incentive behind this comportment lies within the person who acts, and not in the form in which other persons may respond.

To order one's relationships according to the golden rule is to fulfill "the law and the prophets." In effect, this is a fuller expression of God's intention already revealed in the Old Testament. By ordering their actions according to the golden rule, Jesus' disciples move in the direction of the fullest intention of God for the life of His people (see Matthew 5:17). Of course this leads to action which is fully consistent with Jesus' formulation of the great commandment and its complement, "You shall love the Lord your God with all your heart, and with all your soul, and with all your mind. . . . And . . . you shall love your neighbor as yourself" (Matthew 22:37, 39).

In the part of the Sermon on the Mount which follows, Jesus offers four warnings against certain dangers which threaten the life of the community. These are distinguished from the four instructions which appear in the first part of chapter 7 by their increased note of urgency. They deal with dangers which come from outside the community, as well as from within. They do not come in abstract or impersonal forms. They are real dangers in that they represent unacceptable alternatives to the style of life and values described in the Sermon on the Mount which are incorporated in the lives of concrete persons.

### Warnings (Matthew 7:13-27)

*The narrow gate.* The first warning (7:13, 14) which Jesus utters is related to the alternative offered by the "wide gate" and the "easy way." Apparently these are persons outside the community of Jesus whose way of life seems to be as acceptable as it is comfortable. This easy life, together with its corresponding system of values, presents a temptation to many Christians. But what generally goes unnoticed behind the facade of apparent happiness are the problems which cause worry, the dreams which escape fulfillment, the avarice which in reality alienates, the deep loneliness which crowds cannot dissipate, and, finally, self-destruction.

On the other hand, the style of life which is described in the Sermon on the Mount needs to be lived against the stream. The system of values on which life in the messianic community is based is fundamentally opposed to the "easy way" in relation to wealth, the exercise of power, the role of truthfulness, the importance of fidelity, attitude toward wrongdoers, and so on. Although we live in the kingdom of God's grace, it is a life which calls for self-disciplining and accepting mutual responsibility for our discipleship.

The imperative "enter the narrow gate" (13) carries a genuine sense of urgency. This verb—to enter—is frequently used in Matthew's Gospel to designate steps which are particularly decisive. Here it points to the alternative in which a person appropriates the salvation which is offered. It does not mean to enter in the sense of taking the first in a series of many steps along an arduous path, but rather to enter in the sense of simply moving from one sphere to another: into the kingdom (5:20; 7:21; 18:3; 19:23), or into life (18:8; 19:17; cf. 23:13; 25:10). And this "entering" is made possible by the coming of the Messiah.

The image of the "narrow gate" probably does not carry the

idea of a gate which is so small that a person must somehow squeeze through it or stoop to pass beneath its portal. It refers, rather, to the fact that it is so narrow that it is ignored by the majority. In fact, in the last part of verse 14 Jesus says specifically that "those who find it are few." In order to enter the kingdom it is necessary to make a personal choice; stop following the crowds and "find" (14b) and follow Jesus.

The figure of the "hard way" seems to be employed as a synonym for the "narrow gate." It is not a matter of a long path which must be traveled after one has passed through the gate, but, rather, the path into which the narrow gate opens. The essential idea in this figure, just as it was in the case of the "narrow gate," is the fact that the way which leads to life is not the way which the crowds take. When Jesus says that the "way is hard that leads to life" (14) He is, in effect, referring to entrance into the kingdom of heaven (see 7:21).

These verses point to the meaning of following Jesus the Messiah with all of the ethical and spiritual consequences which the militancy in His movement implies. The various calls to repentance (3:2; 4:17; 3:8, 11), and to faith (8:10, 13, 22), and to follow Jesus (10:38; *et al.*), which we find in Matthew's Gospel, all carry the same idea. In His warning Jesus points up the fundamental opposition which exists between the ethic of the "narrow gate" and the "hard way," on one hand, and the "wide gate" and the "easy way," on the other. This warning serves as a reminder to the messianic community of the meaning of its life of discipleship. Of course, it is also pertinent to the community's witness to the gospel, because to follow Jesus is to take the "hard way" and the "narrow gate."

Even more important, here Jesus does not describe a long road to be traveled, at the end of which a person will finally obtain salvation. In reality, salvation is not conceived of apart from life in the kingdom which the Messiah has inaugurated. These verses define Jesus' call to decision, to enter into life, to enter into the kingdom. And having passed through the "narrow gate," one has already arrived at the goal in a very real  anse. Life in the messianic community which Jesus describes in the Sermon on the Mount *is* the form which the salvation that God gives to His people takes, and in it we catch a fleeting but true glimpse of the form it will take when the kingdom comes in all its fullness.

*Dangers within.* The second warning (7:15-20) alerts the messianic community to the dangers which false prophets in their midst represent. The dangers which offer the gravest threat to the church are generally those that come from within. History teaches us that human institutions tend to fail more often from the effects of inner corrosion than due to attacks from the outside. In some ecclesiastical circles there has been the idea that the church evolves toward ever higher expressions of faithfulness and unity. But Jesus, as well as the prophets and the apostles, was more realistic and warned of the possibility of apostasy.

The term translated "beware" (15) is common in Matthew's Gospel as a warning to be on guard against possible deviations from the norm, or perversions in the style of life which corresponds to the messianic community (6:1; 10:17; 16:6). In this case it is a matter of "false prophets" (literally "pseudo prophets"). In the New Testament "pseudo" is used as a prefix together with a wide variety of terms to identify spiritual counterfeiters who appear in the primitive Christian community: "pseudo brothers" (2 Corinthians 11:26; Galatians 2:4), "pseudo apostles" (2 Corinthians 11:15), "pseudo teachers" (2 Peter 2:1), "pseudo witnesses" (Matthew 26:60, 1 Corinthians 15:15), "pseudo messiahs" (Matthew 24:24). In fact, the danger of false prophets has threatened the life of the people of God throughout their history. It was a genuine cause for concern in the Old Testament (Isaiah 9:14; 28:7; Jeremiah 6:13; 8:10; 23:11; Ezekiel 13:3). And from almost the very beginning the Christian church has needed to confront this danger (Matthew 24:11, 24; Acts 13:6; 2 Peter 2:1; 1 John 4:1; Revelation 16:13; 19:20; 20:10).

These false prophets arise within the Christian community. The phrase "come to you" (15) need not be understood in terms of movement from the outside, but rather refers to the fact of their presence, or emergence, in the midst of the community. More often than not, they can scarcely be distinguished from true disciples. In fact, on the surface they seem to be authentic sheep. But eventually the results of their activity betray them and show them up for what they really are.

The figure of a flock of sheep which is applied to the messianic community comes directly from the Old Testament (Psalm 100:3; Ezekiel 34:23; et al.) and it is employed widely in the New Testament. It is noteworthy that the image of "ravenous wolves" (15) to describe the dangers which confront the flock of God is also prominent in the Old Testament (Isaiah 11:6; 66:25; Jeremiah 5:6; Ezekiel 22:27; cf. Acts 20:29, 30). The term which is translated "ravenous" means voracious or greedy in terms of material possessions. In all likelihood, these false prophets were motivated out of greed for gain in snatching the sheep out from under the legitimate authority of the true shepherd. John uses the same term to describe the way in which the "wolf snatches . . . [the sheep] and scatters them" (10:12).

In verses 16-20 the images change to that of a tree and its fruits. In this context the "fruits" undoubtedly refer to the concrete conduct which characterized the false prophets. (See Matthew 3:8, 10; 12:33; 21:43.) But they may also refer to the moral character of the followers which these false prophets gathered around themselves. In other words, the authenticity or spuriousness of a prophet will be recognized in the long run by the moral life of the community which emerges in response to His teachings. We are told twice (16, 20) that the authentic, or the counterfeit character, of the Christian prophet can be judged by the kind of fruits produced. On the other hand, the followers, as well as the ethical comportment of the authentic prophet will reflect the values which are described in the Sermon on the Mount. But in the case of the false prophets this messianic ethic will not be observed.

Verses 16-19 take for granted a concept which our modern mentality finds strange. In reality, a person (in this case the prophet) *is* what he or she *does*, and not what they profess to be or what they say. If they produce good fruit, they are a good tree. If they give bad fruit, they are a bad tree. It is simply inconceivable that a good tree can produce bad fruit, or that a bad tree can give good fruit. The possibility of making a distinction between the fundamental character of a person on one hand, and what that person does on the other hand, corresponds to a modern dualistic concept of personhood. According to the vision presented here, it is impossible to separate between the ethical life of persons and their fundamental character. The modern dualistic distinction does not correspond to the biblical understanding of personhood which sees persons in the integrity of their character manifested in what they do.

*False brethren.* Jesus' third warning (7:21-23) is directed toward false brethren within the community. In these verses it is clear that Jesus expects unconditional obedience to the will of the Father on the part of His disciples. And this will of God is known by all, because it has been revealed by Jesus through His life and teachings (Luke 6:46). Apparently these false brothers were persons in the community who displayed the capacity to transmit messages from God, to do exorcisms and to work other miracles, as well as practicing a seemingly exemplary piety. However, their lives were not clear and unequivocal expressions of the style of life described in the Sermon on the Mount.

But no spiritual accomplishment, no matter how important or desirable it appears to be, can compensate for the absence of a style of life which is consistent with the example and the teachings of Jesus. Without the kind of ethical comportment which, in reality, reflects Jesus' way of being and doing, it is useless to pretend that we are the community of the Messiah—our apparent good intentions, our seemingly valid social concerns, our vision for reform, our ecclesiastical or institutional achievements, our startling messages, and our attention-getting miracles not withstanding.

The phrase, "not every one who says to me, Lord, Lord" (21), refers to a situation in which the follower of Jesus is tempted to turn the demands of discipleship into something which is easier and more attractive. Apparently these are "disciples" whose practice of spirituality attracts the attention of others. The name of the Lord is constantly on their lips (the present tense of the verb "says" points to a practice which has become customary). In fact they rely on pronouncing the "name" to execute their remarkable miracles (22). But Jesus declares that this spirituality is in reality a redundant deception. These persons really do not, nor will they, participate in the kingdom of heaven. Authentic participation in the kingdom is limited to those who do "the will of my Father" (21). And this "will" has been clearly revealed in the person of His Messiah. Jesus not only calls persons to obedience, but through His life and teachings He declares what the content of His obedience is.

"Many" (22) is a term which is frequently employed in Matthew's Gospel to describe those upon whom the judgment of God will come (7:13; 19:30; 22:14). Here it is applied to followers whose dedication to spiritual activism has detracted them from the most elemental demands of the kingdom. (See Matthew 9:13; 12:7; 23:33.) Apparently even the exercise of charismatic gifts (prophesy, exorcisms, and mighty works done in the name of Jesus) is capable of turning many Christians aside from their fundamental duties toward their brothers and sisters, or from their neighbor. Paul also found it necessary to warn that these gifts are vain without love (1 Corinthians 13:2). Those who do not practice the style of life which corresponds to the values of the kingdom, even though they may abound in other expressions of spirituality, are not now, nor will they be on the final day, recognized by their Lord.

The term translated "evil" (23) means literally lawlessness or the absence of law. (The term translated "iniquity" in the parallel passage in Luke 13:27 means the absence of justice.) The evil of these false disciples consists in not listening to their Lord; in disobeying the intention of God, as it has been declared in the teachings of Jesus. The will of God is His "new law" which is declared with authority by His Messiah, the "new Moses."

The "evil" of these false disciples and the "evil fruit" of the false prophets in the preceding verses (15-20) probably carry the same meaning in this context. The only norm by which authentic disciples dare orient their life is that of their Lord, by His Spirit, His words, His actions; in short, according to His style of life. All other shortcuts lead to a dead end.

*Two houses.* Jesus directs His fourth warning (7:24-27) toward those who do not put into practice the new law of the kingdom which He has given in the Sermon on the Mount. The parable of the two houses makes it clear that Jesus intended that the teachings included in the Sermon on the Mount should be obeyed. The new law of the kingdom has been announced for all those who have begun to experience the joy of the messianic age—those who are described in the beatitudes. But this does not mean that its teachings can be taken with any less seriousness. To pretend to be citizens of the new world which the Messiah has ushered in without putting into practice Jesus' teachings is utter folly. The total ruin of those who do not practice the instructions of Jesus is announced to them here.

In this context the phrase, "every one then who hears these words of mine and does them" (24) refers to the followers of Jesus who have responded enthusiastically to the Master and have begun to put into practice, not only His teachings in general, but quite specifically, the Sermon on the Mount. (This is clearly the impression which Matthew's arrangement of Jesus' teachings in his Gospel gives.) The "wise man" (24) is not merely an expression which describes the quality of a person's soul or spirit. Here the term refers to a person's concrete ethical comportment. The wise person is one who knows what should be done and does it. In the biblical tradition to be wise, or prudent, is to believe *and* to obey. It implies both hearing and doing. In effect, Jesus tells us that persons construct their life by putting into practice what they have heard, just as one builds a house by carrying out the prescribed procedures. To build "upon a rock" in this case is to put into practice "these words" of Jesus (24).

In this case, the torrential rains, together with the flooding which they produce, as well as the hurricane-like winds which put the recent construction to the test, are simply proofs that the house is well built (25). The firmness of the person who puts Jesus' words to practice will be demonstrated in the hour of testing.

But the very opposite is the case of the "foolish man" who does not put into practice these words of Jesus (26). The folly of the "foolish man" does not consist in his not listening to the words of Jesus, nor in his not having perceived their importance. In fact, the context seems to indicate that he delighted himself in them spiritually. His madness lies in the fact that he has heard them without doing them.

In the light of the Christian church's history this parable calls us to serious reflection. The beatitudes with which Jesus described the essential character of those who participate in the kingdom have had a limited impact on the life of the church as a whole. They have generally found expression only within marginal groups within Christendom. The radical new dimensions which Jesus gave to the ancient law of God have gone largely unnoticed in the church's practice. Anger in interpersonal relationships, infidelity in marital relationships, falsehood in social relationships, vengeance toward the offender, and hatred of one's enemies have been left behind by an ethic of self-giving love which responds more exactly to God's real intention for human life together. But this fact has found little echo in the institutional church. For the vast majority of Christians the ethic of Jesus represents a goal which is altogether unrealistic. Therefore, the regulation of marital problems by means of divorce, the limitation of falsehood through the swearing of oaths to be truthful, the limitation of vengeance by legal restrictions on retaliation, and keeping violence from getting entirely out of control by the doctrines of legitimate self-defense and the just war is about as high a level of morality as can be expected from most modern Christians.

Jesus warns against hypocrisy in the practice of our spirituality, but religiosity, unaccompanied by a corresponding growth in serious ethical commitment, is on the increase in the church.

Jesus warned against the anxious laying up of "treasures on earth," but Christians in the Northern and Western hemispheres (where traditional Christianity is largely to be found) continue to enrich themselves at the expense of the poor and hungry of the world. Jesus warned against those merely spiritualistic expressions of faith which are unconcerned about the fundamental questions of social justice and self-giving love, but this shallow uncommitted spirituality continues to spread. Jesus warned against the folly of indulging oneself in the spiritual delights of religious language without the accompanying practice of obedience. But, where are those who are willing to build their "house upon the rock"?

### Questions for Discussion

1. Why are Christians sometimes tempted to "pass judgment" on one another? What is the antidote for this problem?

2. Do you agree that our defensive mechanisms do not even allow us to see our own defects, let alone correct them? Does this mean then that we are absolutely dependent on our brothers and sisters for the kind of discipline which will allow us to grow in our discipleship?

3. You may know of persons who, by all appearances, attempt to practice the Sermon on the Mount without the resource of the Holy Spirit. On the other hand, you may know Christians who claim the Holy Spirit, but whose lives are not best described by the Sermon on the Mount. Has it been your experience that the Holy Spirit releases amazing resources for living according to the values of the kingdom?

4. Can you think of two or three concrete results of applying the "golden rule" in interpersonal relationships in your congregation? Would this lead in the direction of the kind of kingdom living described in the Sermon on the Mount?

5. Do you agree that the Sermon on the Mount describes the concrete social contours of salvation experienced in Christ's community? If so, what does this mean in relation to the other "ways" which commend themselves to Christians?

6. Are there sure criteria for evaluating the claims of the "Christian voices" of our time? If so, what are some of these criteria and how do these "voices" pass the test?

7. Many Christians in our time tend to emphasize either spiritual experience or sound doctrine as the prime key for measuring the authenticity of the Christian life. How do you think authenticity should

be measured? What clues for our search does Matthew 7 offer? What does the history of the Christian church contribute (both negatively and positively) to our understanding of what is essential to the life of the messianic community?

8. Would you say the life of the messianic community described in the Sermon on the Mount is utopic? Or, are you finding it to be a joyful, saving possibility?

# Chapter 8

# Conclusion
# (Matthew 7:28, 29)

The words with which Matthew begins his conclusion, "and when Jesus finished these sayings," are not intended to imply that these are all of Jesus' teachings, nor that they are necessarily the most important of His instructions. They simply mean that this particular collection of Jesus' teachings which Matthew has brought together for a specific purpose is ended. In addition to Jesus' teachings concerning the righteousness of the kingdom contained in the Sermon on the Mount, Matthew includes in his Gospel four other collections: instructions to the messengers of the kingdom (chapter 10), parables which reveal the mystery of the kingdom (chapter 13), instructions on the exercise of discipline in the messianic community (chapter 18), and teachings concerning the final appearing of the kingdom (chapters 24, 25).

The "astonishment" of the multitudes at Jesus' teachings was not due simply to an enthusiastic embrace, for sentimental or intellectual reasons, of a convincing presentation. They were moved, rather, by the question of fundamental concern for every Jew of the period: is this the Messiah? Does the teaching of Jesus carry the authority of God Himself who is thus revealing Himself to His people? In effect, this is the meaning of the word "authority" (29). The "authority" with which Jesus acted and spoke constituted a problem to His hearers (Matthew 21:23; Mark 1:22; Luke 4:32). He spoke with the authority of a rabbi, though He had not been taught or ordained. His authority was therefore not derivative but autonomous. His authority was plainly not like that of "their scribes" (29).

Jesus was in their midst "as one who had authority" (29). In Jesus' own person and ministry the reign of God had drawn near. Therefore, the authority with which He spoke was God's authority. In effect, Matthew answers the prime Jewish question of the time—is this the Messiah?—affirmatively by pointing to the authority with which Jesus taught.

This explains why Jesus could present God's intention for human life together in all of its original radicality and simplicity. No wonder the crowds were astonished! No wonder these words are to be taken with such seriousness by the messianic community—through whom God continues to exercise His authority to the end of the age.

# Epilogue

Utopia is, by definition, a place which does not exist. And for the vast majority of modern Christians the instructions of Jesus contained in the Sermon on the Mount appear to create such a utopia. For them the kingdom of God which Jesus came to establish cannot happen within human history. At best, it is the object of a faraway hope that will become reality at the last great day, in the final consummation.

But the way of life which is described in these chapters is not utopia. They describe the way of peace and justice which was practiced by the Messiah. They describe the values which oriented life in the primitive apostolic community. This system of values, and the style of life which grows out of it, is presupposed by all of the New Testament documents and is essential for their interpretation and understanding.

The apostles remembered Jesus as the One who incarnated perfectly these values, this style of life in their midst. These are precisely the same values which oriented the new life of the messianic community. These are the values which the apostles commend to all those who are touched by the grace of God and join themselves to the messianic movement. Gentiles as well as Jews are invited to experience this new life of love in that community which is already a participant of the power of the age to come, and anticipates already in its life the righteousness which will characterize the kingdom when it comes in all its fullness.

Throughout the long course of the history of the Christian church, communities of the followers of Jesus have emerged which, by the power of His Spirit, have oriented their life in the values of the kingdom which Jesus brought. In fact, in our own time we have personally known men and women, young and old, whose lives are clearly guided by these values and by the Spirit who inspires them. It is true their number is relatively small, but their presence in the church and in the world is like a cool breeze on a sweltering summer day. Their lives are like lights in the midst of dense darkness. They are like salt which seasons an otherwise insipid human existence. They are the messianic community present in the world today.

Some of them are to be found in the institutional church, but they are wary lest they be tempted to trust in worldly forms of power for their salvation. They all lead a more or less precarious existence in the midst of society, because they are all oriented in the opposite direction. Spiritually and socially and economically, they have to swim against the current. In fact, in some places they are obliged to survive incognito because of their self-giving in the cause of Christ. Others are hailed before the courts and imprisoned for the cause of justice. But all of them have one thing in common. They are all oriented by the Spirit of their Lord and their daily lives are faithful reflections of His.

Far from being a utopia, the reign of God takes form today wherever His people live the life of the kingdom by faith, and in the power of His Holy Spirit. It is the life of the kingdom, lived to its fullest one time by Jesus of Nazareth, described in the clearest of terms in the Sermon on the Mount, practiced obediently by the primitive apostolic community, and undertaken by groups of disciples throughout the centuries in spite of the demonic pressures of this present evil age.

This is the life of the kingdom of God already present in our midst, which, by the marvelous grace of God, will one day embrace the whole universe.

Utopia? No! It is the only realistic way to live today in the light of the glorious tomorrow which is coming to meet us!

**John Driver** grew up in Hesston, Kansas, where he graduated from Hesston Academy. He received his BA from Goshen College, Goshen, Indiana, in 1950, his BD from Goshen Biblical Seminary in 1960, and his STM from Perkins School of Theology, Dallas, Texas, in 1967. He married Bonita Landis. They are the parents of Cynthia, Wilfred, and Jonathan.

The Drivers have been working as part of the Mennonite Board of Missions (Elkhart, Indiana) Latin team since 1951. Earlier, John served with Mennonite Central Committee (MCC) and Mennonite Relief Committee in Puerto Rico from 1945 to 1948 and Bonita served from 1947 to 1948. They then worked as missionaries in Puerto Rico from 1951 to 1966 and in Uruguay from 1967 to 1974.

As part of his missionary assignment in Uruguay, John Driver was professor of church history and New Testament at the Seminario Evangelico Menonita de Teologia, Montevideo. He also served the seminary until its closing in late 1974 as dean of studies from 1967, and as acting rector from 1972. Since 1975 the

Drivers have spent most of their time establishing a Mennonite witness in Spain.

John Driver is coauthor with Samuel Escobar of *Christian Mission and Social Justice* (Herald Press, 1978). He also wrote *Community and Commitment* (Herald Press, 1976) which first appeared as *Comunidad y Compromiso* in Argentina in 1974.